Enneagram:

An Introduction to Self-Discovery

By Cindy Webber

Table of Contents

Introduction

Congratulations on downloading this book and thank you for doing so.

The following chapters will discuss how the philosophy of the Enneagram personality types came to be accepted, what you need to know about each personality type and how they interact with each other. You will learn how you can leverage the power of your strengths to improve your life.

What is the Enneagram?

The Enneagram (pronounced any-a-gram) means nine-pointed line drawing in Greek, and that's exactly what the Enneagram structure looks like. Nine points are spaced equal distance along the circumference of a circle and connected by a triangle and a 6-pointed line drawing. The lines are connected in a way that shows relationship between the personality types during periods of stress and periods of growth (security).

Enneagram History

The shape of the Enneagram itself has ancient origins. However, personality types have just been applied to the nine positions in the last fifty years.

George Gurdjieff
The Enneagram symbol as it appears today was first used by
George I. Gurdjieff in the early 20th century. Gurdjieff used the
numbers to understand steps in a process as it moved around
the circle. He referenced the Enneagram diagram in his dance
training. He was also known to point out different types of
people but not necessarily grouped with the nine points as they
are today. He also recognized the mental, emotional, and
instinctual centers that comprise wholeness in people. He
recognized the importance of these three centers to become
well-balanced.

Oscar Ichazo
Sometime during the 50s and 60s Oscar Ichazo placed ego-types
upon the Enneagram symbol. Each ego-type was defined by a
fixation and remedied by a holy idea. Each ego-type was also
defined by a passion and remedied by a virtue.

Claudio Naranjo
Around 1970 a psychiatrist named Claudio Naranjo learned
about Ichazo's ego-types. Naranjo mapped the ego-types to DSM
personality syndromes. Some types fit well, others not so well,
and some fit more than one syndrome. During the 70s, Naranjo
evolved the types into the personality types of the Enneagram
(Ennea-Types). It was directly from Naranjo's Ennea-types that
Enneagram Personality Types developed.

Power of the number Three
The number three has been quite significant to humans
throughout history. A complete thought or process is comprised
of a beginning, middle, and end. In writing, we have our
introduction, body, and conclusion. Many religions consider
three higher powers. When we think of wholeness of health, we
consider our body, our head, and our heart. The Enneagram
enforces the idea of the power of the number three. Nine is the
square of three, or 3 x 3. Each personality type represented by
the Enneagram is also influenced by three parts: the wing
personality, the stress point of a personality type, and the
security point of a personality type. Each of the three points is
located within each of the three centers powered by the head,
heart, or body.

Enneagram Philosophy

The philosophy of the Enneagram structure and personality types is based on spiritual and ancient Greek philosophies. It is based on the fundamental beliefs there is good and bad for everyone. It also shares the belief that one type would not be complete without qualities of at least three other types. Some people, including Claudio Naranjo, believe everyone exhibits features from each personality type. Others believe people go through different types as they develop through life. For example, your primary type before age 25 may not be your primary type in your 40s. The purpose of the Enneagram personality types is not to just tell you, "This is why you act the way you do, accept it." Instead, it helps you understand yourself and your type better so you can adapt to your strengths and weaknesses. The Enneagram philosophy will give you a foundation to work on improving yourself and know how to overcome your weaknesses and cope with others in their weakness.

Chapter 1: An Introduction to the Enneagram Personalities

The Enneagram structure is set up like a clock with only 9 numbers. Nine is on the top with Type One to the right and counting up in a clockwise-manner.

The Enneagram Personalities are based on three main centers: The Body (Instinct-Based), The Heart (Emotional-Based), and The Head (Intellectual-Based).

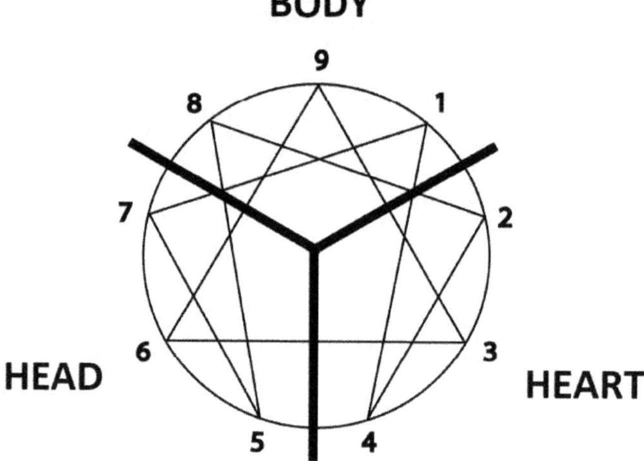

The Body personality types include: Type 8, Type 9, and Type 1.
    Type 8 is often referred to as The Challenger.
    Type 9 is often referred to as The Peacemaker.
    Type 1 is often referred to as The Reformer.

The Heart personality types include: Type 2, Type 3, and Type 4.
    Type 2 is often referred to as The Helper.
    Type 3 is often referred to as The Achiever.
    Type 4 is often referred to as The Individualist.

The Head personality types include: Type 5, Type 6, and Type 7.
    Type 5 is often referred to as The Investigator.
    Type 6 is often referred to as The Loyalist.
    Type 7 is often referred to as The Enthusiast.

Each type breaks down into subsets based on the wing personalities. Many people will lean strongly toward one of the neighboring personality types.

Therefore, Type 9 people can either be Type 9 wing 8 or Type 9 wing 1. Type 1 people can either be Type 1 wing 9 or Type 1 wing 2.

In addition to wing types, each type has a corresponding stress point and a corresponding security (growth) point. When a person is under stress, one may demonstrate the weakness of his/her personality type's stress point. During times of growth and security, one may demonstrate the strengths of his/her personality type's security point.

Stress points

The arrows point to each personality type's stress point.

Type 1 will get negative traits from Type 4 during times of stress.

Type 2 will get negative traits from Type 8 during times of stress.

Type 3 will get negative traits from Type 9 during times of stress.

Type 4 will get negative traits from Type 2 during times of stress.

Type 5 will get negative traits from Type 7 during times of stress.

Type 6 will get negative traits from Type 3 during times of stress.

Type 7 will get negative traits from Type 1 during times of stress.

Type 8 will get negative traits from Type 5 during times of stress.

Type 9 will get negative traits from Type 6 during times of stress.

Security Points

The arrows point to each personality type's security point. When people are comfortable and ready for growth in their life, they may get positive traits from their security type.

Type 1 will receive positive traits from Type 7 during times of growth.

Type 2 will receive positive traits from Type 4 during times of growth.

Type 3 will receive positive traits from Type 6 during times of growth.

Type 4 will receive positive traits from Type 1 during times of growth.

Type 5 will receive positive traits from Type 8 during times of growth.

Type 6 will receive positive traits from Type 9 during times of growth.

Type 7 will receive positive traits from Type 5 during times of growth.

Type 8 will receive positive traits from Type 2 during times of growth.

Type 9 will receive positive traits from Type 3 during times of growth.

The path of movement is opposite between stress and security points.

Chapter 2: Type 1 – The Reformer

The Type One Reformers are always on a mission to improve the world. They strive to overcome adversity. They are also known for being perfectionists. Ones are activists searching for acceptable reasoning for their missions of what they feel they must do to improve the world.

People who have Type One personality are meticulous and ethical. They have a strong sense of what is right and acceptable and what is wrong or unacceptable. Many Type One people become teachers, activists, and advocates for change. Their goal is to improve the world and people around them and avoid making any mistakes. They are orderly, well-organized, and can be demanding of the people around them. They try to maintain high standards which can cause them to be critical of others and come off as a perfectionist. They typically have problems with resentment and impatience. Type Ones are discerning, noble, realistic, and wise at their best. They have high respect for moral standards and live up to those standards better than most people.

As a perfectionist, the possibility of being wrong is a tremendous concern and fear for a Type One personality. Their basic desire is to be balanced, have integrity, and an overall sense of doing what is good and right.

The most notable One personalities are those who have left behind comfortable lifestyles for the better good of others. They chase extraordinary adventures and do extraordinary accomplishments for the betterment of others. Even Type Ones on a lesser level still desire to be useful to others and to the environment.

On a more negative level, Type Ones are constantly justifying their actions to themselves and to others.

Ones are constantly beating themselves up for mistakes or wrongdoings.

If you are a Type One who is constantly listening to the unforgiving and nagging voice in your subconscious, learn to separate your self-worth from that voice. Instead, learn from the mistakes, accept that you cannot be perfect all the time and you will be able to use your inner voice for growth.

A Type One personality with a Nine-wing is more idealistic. They may use their ideas to justify their behavior. Their fear of being condemned by anyone turns them away from criticism. A Type One with a Two-wing becomes an advocate. They know the best ways to help others and improve their environment.

Stress Point

When Type Ones are stressed. They may show unhealthy level traits of Type Four personalities.

Some of these unhealthy traits may include:

- Depression
- Avoidance
- Narcissism
- Despair
- Feelings of hopeless
- Shame

Security Point

When Type Ones experience periods of growth, they may show average to healthy level traits of Type Seven personalities.

Some of these healthy traits may include:

- Grateful
- Appreciative
- Joyous
- Demonstrate goodness of life
- Enthusiastic
- Extroverted
- Practical
- Productive

Type 1 Levels of Development

Levels 1,2 and 3 are considered healthy levels of development. Remember that the traits exhibited in these levels can also be seen by Type Fours during their times of growth.

Levels 3, 4 and 5 are considered average levels of development.

Levels 6, 7 and 8 are considered unhealthy levels of development. Remember that the traits exhibited in these levels can also be seen by Type Sevens during times of stress.

Healthy:

Level 1
Extraordinary wisdom and discernment
They begin to understand what is actually realistic and know the best course of action to take in each situation.

Level 2
Reliable personal convictions
Their sense of right and wrong aligns with their religious and moral values. They desire to be reasonable, rational, self-disciplined, achieve balance and maturity in all things.

Level 3
High principles
They strive to be ethical, fair, and objective. Justice and truth are their primary values. Their sense of purpose, responsibility, and integrity help them teach others and witness to the truth.

Average:

Level 4
Idealist critics, crusaders, and advocates.
They are not satisfied with reality. It becomes their personal mission to improve everything. These are the people constantly serving multiple causes. They have a strong sense of how they feel things should be.

Level 5
Afraid of making mistakes

Everything must be consistent with their ideals. They are well-organized but impersonal and emotionally distant. They don't let their feelings or impulses show or control their actions in any way. They are workaholics, punctual, and demanding.

Level 6
Judgmental perfectionists
They are very opinionated about everything causing them to be highly critical of themselves and those around them. They constantly scold people who will never be able to live up to their standards of perfection. They can come across as abrasive and angry

Unhealthy:

Level 7
Dogmatic
They are inflexible, intolerant, and self-righteous. They believe they are the only one who can be right. They are strict in judgment but rationalize their own actions.

Level 8
Hypocritical
They obsess over the imperfections and mistakes of others, but they are blind to their own actions.

Level 9
Obsessive-compulsive disorder and depressive personality disorders are common mental health issues. They may experience severe depression or nervous breakdowns. They push others away to separate themselves from the imperfections of others.

Chapter 3: Type Two – The Helper

People who have a Type Two personality are labeled as helpers because they are warm-hearted and empathetic. Their goal is to help people and serve others while sometimes neglecting their own needs.

Type Twos genuinely try their best to help others whenever they can, but they also love to be recognized as being helpful.

They feel sharing love and concern for others is the best way to live. Family and friendship are especially important to type Two personalities.

Type twos are understanding and compassionate. They have seemingly unlimited patience and are always willing to help out. A healthy Two will know how and when to let go of people in their life, while unhealthier type Twos have a hard time letting go and insist on being needed.

People are drawn to type Twos and many times take advantage of type Two's generosity.

They are well-meaning but sometimes their drive to help others becomes a need to be needed. They often have problems recognizing and admitting their own needs.

Their basic desire to feel loved leads to a central fear of being unwanted or unworthy of love.

Type Twos' development may be hindered by their tendency to become over-
involved in the lives of those around them.

Self-development requires visiting dark places in our subconscious – a place Type Twos avoid. They prefer to see themselves as completely positive and full of light.

The biggest obstacle for Type Twos (along with Threes and Fours centered around a common sense of shame) is facing their fear of being worthless to others. They feel they are nothing without their great acts of service.

Unhealthy Twos validate their self-worth by how much of themselves they sacrifice for others. They trade generosity and over-involvement as a means to obtain the love they secretly desire.

Type Twos with a One-wing may fall into the role of a servant. They direct their need to be needed to serving others, many times to a fault.

Type Twos with a Three-wing may serve the role of a host/hostess. They enjoy being able to bring people closer together.
Stress Point

When Type Twos are stressed, they may exhibit negative or unhealthy levels of development typically seen in Type Eight personalities.

These unhealthy traits include:

- Vengeful
- Murderous
- Sociopathic
- Callous
- Hard-hearted
- Antisocial
- Totalitarianism
- Feel invincible
- Reckless
- Dictatorial
- Immoral
- Violent
- Confrontational
- Threatening
- Proud
- Domineering

- Self-sufficient

Security Point

During times of growth Type Twos may exhibit positive or healthy levels of development typically seen in Type Fours personalities.

These healthy traits include:

- Creative
- Inspired
- Self-aware
- Sensitive to others
- Gentle
- Tactful
- Compassionate
- Individualistic
- Humane

Levels of Development

Healthy:

Level 1
Humble
Healthy level Twos are unselfish and altruistic. They have unconditional love to offer others. They consider it a privilege to be involved in the lives of others.

Level 2
Compassionate
Type Twos in this stage of development have sincere empathy for the feelings of others. They truly care about the needs of others. They are sincere, warm-hearted, thoughtful and forgiving towards others.

Level 3
Encouraging

They see the good in others. This level of development remembers to take care of their self as well as others. They are nurturing and generous in their giving – a truly loving person.

Average:

Level 4
People-pleasers
In an attempt to please the people around them, Twos may try to show off their loving nature and attempt to become too close to people.

Level 5
Overly intrusive
They develop a need to be needed. They try to meddle and control the lives of others in the name of love. They start to become codependent and self-sacrificial. They believe they can never do enough for others.

Level 6
Overbearing
They become a "martyr" for others. They may overrate their efforts for the benefit of others. They believe they are indispensable, other people need them. At times, they may be patronizing and presumptuous.

Unhealthy:

Level 7
Manipulative
Level 7 Type Two are self-serving. They tell people how much the other person "owes" them. They may abuse food or drugs to "stuff their feelings" and get sympathy from the people around them. They may make belittling remarks to undermine people. They are self-deceptive about how damaging their behavior and motives are.

Level 8
Coercive
This stage of Twos may become domineering. They feel they are entitled to repayment for all the service they gave to others.

Level 9
Victims

They rationalize their behavior by becoming victims. They are angry and resentful toward others. Many people in this stage resemble or become Hypochondriacs. They use health problems real, or imagined, to get attention.

Chapter 4: Type Three – The Achiever

Type Threes are success-oriented and practical. They are driven and adapt to the situation as needed so they can excel in everything they do. Threes are concerned with how people perceive them. They want others to see them as competent to get the job done.

Threes are self-assured and ambitious. However, they also have a charming sense of energy. They are highly driven for advancement in their positions. Threes are poised and diplomatic. They want to make every aspect of their life a success and a model for others.

Healthy Threes are more than capable of achieving great things to change the world. People look up to them because of their accomplishments and their graciousness. Healthy Threes feel good developing and contributing their abilities to those around them. They enjoy motivating others to work hard and see how much they can accomplish.

These are your typical workaholics and competitors. To other people, they may be considered the "teacher's pet" or a "brown-noser." They can be seen going out of their way to stay over at work and skipping breaks to get a job done. They work extremely well under pressure.

Their basic desire to feel worthwhile and valuable can instill a fear of being worthless. Threes may become so consumed with other people's definition of success they lose sight of who they really are. They pursue success for other people rather than personal gain.

Threes perceive emotions as a roadblock to success. Being in tune with their own desires might make them lose respect from others. Therefore, they box up their feelings and interests, in an attempt to appear successful. This need to drown their feelings is usually fueled by their childhood.

They were pressured to believe they were nobody and worthless unless they excelled in certain areas. Many people receive the same type of message, but Threes really take it to heart the most. When confronted with the question, "What do I personally want from life?" They generally do not have an answer because they were never allowed to explore their own interests.

Threes with a Two-wing may be classified as "The Charmer," while Threes with a Four-wing are classified as "The Professional."

Threes have a strong need for affirmation and rewards. They expect acknowledgement of their achievements and may feel used and undervalued when they are not acknowledged for their work.

Stress Point
When Type Threes are stressed, they may exhibit negative or unhealthy levels of development typically seen in Type Nine personalities.
These unhealthy traits include:

- Withdrawn
- Numb
- Stubborn
- Neglectful
- "Peace at any cost"
- Tune out reality
- Idealize others

Security Point
During times of growth Type Threes may exhibit positive or healthy levels of development typically seen in Type Six personalities.
These healthy traits include:

- Independent
- Cooperative
- Endearing
- Responsible

- Hard-working
- Persevering

Levels of Development

Healthy:

Level 1
Self-accepting
Threes are authentically modest, charitable, gentle, and benevolent toward helping others. They are full of heart and humor others by putting themselves down.

Level 2
Self-assured
Threes have high self-esteem and know how competent they are. They have confidence in their self-worth. They are charming and gracious. Others desire them because they adapt well to any situation.

Level 3
Ambitious
Threes will do anything to improve themselves into becoming the "best them." They are outstanding role models, and others become motivated to mirror them in positive ways.

Average:

Level 4
High performance
Threes are terrified of failing. They strive for excellence and success. Their self-worth diminishes if they aren't the best.

Level 5
Image-conscious
At this stage, Threes are fully concerned with their reputation and how others perceive them. They begin to lose touch with their feelings and ideas.

Level 6
Narcissistic

They may exaggerate their accomplishments and embellish their strengths. At this point, they become arrogant in their attempt to seek attention and acknowledgment.

Unhealthy:

Level 7
Manipulative
They envy the success others and are willing to fudge ethics to gain an edge. They may lie and cheat to gain promotions.

Level 8
Devious
Unhealthy Threes will become malicious towards others. They will sabotage other people's chance for success.

Level 9
Vindictive
They become relentless in ruining other's happiness. They become obsessed with destroying evidence of their failures.

Chapter 5: Type Four – The Individualist

Fours are sensitive and introspective. They can be dramatic and expressive about the situations happening in their life. They can also be self-absorbed and temperamental.

Fours are very self-aware which can also make them feel self-conscious of their faults. They dwell on the characteristics that make them defective and what they can do to create an identity separate from those around them. They typically have a negative self-image and low self-esteem.

While they tend to be emotionally honest and personal, their self-consciousness can also make them more reserved. They may withdraw from others when they become vulnerable and feel defective.

They want to be extraordinary and have great disdain for living ordinary lifestyles. This causes them to have problems with their self-worth when melancholy and self-indulgence creep in, developing a sense of self-pity.
On a positive note, Fours are highly creative and inspired. They use their creativity to transform experiences. They are able to use inspiration to renew their spirits.

Fours true desire is to find their identity and discover every aspect of their personality. Fours typically feel as if they are lacking, but they usually can't pinpoint exactly what they feel they lack in. Their biggest fear is not being able to leave behind a significant legacy for others to remember them by.

They want to be seen as an individualist that can stand out in a crowd. In a relationship, they desire someone who will appreciate the identity they have created. Fours need someone who sees them as unique and appreciates their uniqueness even more than they do.

Healthy Fours can own up to their feelings and appreciate the little things that make them unique. They are not ashamed of their setbacks and weaknesses. They would rather embrace their true identity even if they don't like what they see.

Lower level Fours may create a "Fantasy Self-Image" of who they want to be. In their mind, they may embellish their skills and abilities. However, when asked to perform these special skills, they become embarrassed because the truth doesn't match their fantasy.

The harshness they put on themselves does allow them to endure painful experiences better than other types. Fours may hang on their negativities until it starves them of happiness. They won't recognize their treasures until they stop putting themselves down and start living up to positive affirmations. Fours with a Three-Wing are seen as "The Aristocrat," while Fours with a Five-wing are seen as "The Bohemian."

Stress Point
When Type Fours are stressed, they may exhibit negative or unhealthy levels of development typically seen in Type Two personalities.

These unhealthy traits include:

- People-pleaser
- Intrusive
- Presumptuous
- Manipulative
- Domineering
- Victimized

Security Point
During times of growth Type Fours may exhibit positive or healthy levels of development typically seen in Type One personalities.

These healthy traits include:

- Wise
- Discerning

- Conscientious
- Principled
- Responsible
- Ethical

Levels of Development

Healthy:

Level 1
Creative
Fours express themselves and their perceived universe through art. They transform their situations into valuable learning experiences.

Level 2
Introspective
They are aware of their personal feeling and attributes. They can be sensitive to themselves. They are tactful, gentle, and compassionate toward others.

Level 3
Individualistic
They are able to reveal their emotions honestly. They have an ironic view on life. They can be both serious and funny. They may be emotionally strong but also vulnerable.

Average:

Level 4
Imaginative
They use their fantasies to beautify their life.

Level 5
Hypersensitive
They may become too in touch with feelings. They take everything personally. They may become introverted and self-conscious.

Level 6
Self-pity

They are impractical in their view of their lifestyle. They feel they are exempt from living like an "ordinary" person. They envy those with more exciting lifestyle, becoming self-indulgent to their wants.

Unhealthy:

Level 7
Ashamed
Fours are ashamed of themselves when their plans fail. They get depressed and alienate from the world so they don't have to see what they should have been.

Level 8
Contempt
They are surrounded in a personal hell, being tormented by their thoughts. They blame others around them for their failure and drive away those who try to help.

Level 9
Despair
Unhealthy Fours are prone to emotional breakdowns. They begin to feel hopeless, finding addictions to help them escape their personal torment.

Chapter 6: Type Five – The Investigator

Fives are intense and intellectual. They can be perceptive and innovative. But, they can also be secretive and isolated.

Fives are insightful, curious, and alert. They enjoy solving mental puzzles. Fives are innovative and inventive, but they prefer to be independent. They tend to get lost in their mind contemplating solutions.

Despite becoming detached from society, Fives can be high-strung and intense. They develop problems with nihilism, eccentricity, and isolation. Many times, they focus too much energy on academic knowledge. They neglect developing social and practical skills.

In a positive light, Fives are visionary pioneers. They are considered "ahead of their time" because they have the ability to see the world and situations they encounter in a unique way. Fives are not turned on by the tried and true. Instead, they want to be the ones to discover uncharted territory, to be the first to know something. Many Fives will find one special niche they feel they can master.
Fives are motivated to learn as much as they can about the world around them.

They plan everything and use knowledge to protect themselves from setbacks.
Fives fear being useless, so they develop their mental capacity to devise enlightening solutions to complicated problems. They do not believe they have unique skills to offer. So, they use their research skills to learn new skills, so they have something to contribute to the world. They may use their knowledge and observations to invent something useful. Their contributions make them feel valuable as a person, but they want to be careful to wait until they know it works.

Fives are considered investigators because they strive to explore and learn as much as they can about how and why things are the way they are in natures. They even investigate their own feelings and imaginations. However, they are also the world's toughest skeptics. In an attempt to learn and explain as much as they can about the inner workings of life, they question everyone's theories until they are confident in their beliefs.

Type Fives with a Four-wing may be considered eccentric, while type Fives with a Six-wing are problem solvers.

Stress Point
When Type Fives are stressed, they may exhibit negative or unhealthy levels of development typically seen in Type Seven personalities.

These unhealthy traits include:

- Bipolar
- Erratic mood swings
- Impulsive
- Demanding
- Uninhibited
- Adventurous

Security Point
During times of growth Type Fives may exhibit positive or healthy levels of development typically seen in Type Eight personalities.

These healthy traits include:

- Self-restrained
- Merciful
- Resourceful
- Decisive
- Authoritative
- Self-confident
- Self-sufficient

Levels of Development

Healthy:

Level 1
Visionary
Fives who are open-minded can make pioneering discoveries. Their capacity for new knowledge is limitless.

Level 2
Observationist
They are mentally alert and focused. Their curiosity leads them to more knowledge.

Level 3
Knowledge Master
They study their chosen field until they become "master of their domain."

Average:

Level 4
Studious
They become obsessed with making sure all their theories are accurate and fit together. Blueprints and models fill their offices.

Level 5
Detached
They become preoccupied with off-beat subjects that do not pertain to the practical world.

Level 6
Antagonistic
Fives become cynical and abrasive toward anyone who does not accept their views.

Unhealthy:

Level 7
Reclusive

They become fearful of aggression and rejection of their ideas, so they separate from social engagements.

Level 8
Phobic
They become obsessed with the dangers of the world and develop crazy phobias. If there's a one in a million chance being in danger by something they will fear it.

Level 9
Schizophrenic
By this point, Fives have had a devastating break from reality. They become deranged by their imaginations and abhor truth.

Chapter 7 - Type Six – The Loyalist

Sixes are committed to others and focused on safety and security. Healthy Sixes can be engaging and responsible. Lower functioning Sixes become anxious and suspicious.

Sixes are hard-working, reliable, trustworthy, and responsible. They are able to anticipate problems and react quickly to help solve problems. At times, they may become too cautious, resulting in indecisiveness.

Sixes are too involved in their thoughts and the what-ifs to have confidence in their decisions. They begin to worry about what could happen. Most of the time, the scenarios in their mind are much worse than the reality of what is most likely to happen.

When the problems become more than they can handle, Sixes become anxious. They combat their anxiety by being defensive and evasive.

Sixes struggle with suspicion and self-doubt. Their self-doubt stems from their lack of confidence in themselves. They need support and guidance from others to feel secure in their choices.

Sixes are loyal to a fault. They hang on to relationships for better or for worse, many times too much for the worse. They stick around for the long-haul even when the relationship is strained and even if they have to suffer personally. They will fight for their beliefs, their family, and their community more than their own personal needs.

While most Sixes go with the flow and loyal to other's beliefs and ideas, some Sixes may try to step out and be revolutionary or even rebellious.

Sixes can be defined by their contradictory manner.

Depending on their situation, Sixes can be:

- Strong and weak

- Trusting and distrusting
- Fearful and courageous
- Defenders and provokers
- Sweet and sour
- Bully and weak
- Aggressive and passive
- Defensive and offensive
- Social and loner
- Believers and doubters
- Tender and mean
- Cooperative and obstructive
- Generous and petty

Sixes must learn to face their anxieties and personal issues before they can become courageous and serene in any and all circumstances.

Sixes with a Five-Wing are known as "The Defender," while Sixes with a Seven-wing are known as "The Buddy."

Stress Point
When Type Sixes are stressed, they may exhibit negative or unhealthy levels of development typically seen in Type Three personalities.

These unhealthy traits include:

- Image-Conscious
- Narcissistic
- Manipulative
- Devious
- Vindictive

Security Point
During times of growth Type Sixes may exhibit positive or healthy levels of development typically seen in Type Nine personalities.

These healthy traits include:

- Independent
- Self-sufficient
- Patient
- Self-effacing
- Optimistic

Levels of Development

Healthy:

Level 1
Self-affirming
High functioning Sixes have confidence in themselves that creates courage and self-expression.

Level 2
Lovable
They are able to gain emotional responses from others by being seen as endearing and affectionate. They build trust that leads to permanent relationships and alliances.

Level 3
Dedicated
They work hard for the causes they believe in. Their friends and family can rely on Sixes to be there for them. They create an environment of security and stability.

Average:

Level 4
Vigilant
They start to lose trust in their own opinions and look to others for stable solutions. They are on alert for potential problems.

Level 5
Passive-aggressive
They may become evasive and indecisive to resist adding responsibilities to their plate. Many of these Sixes are procrastinators.

Level 6
Sarcastic
To compensate for insecurities, they blame others for their own problems. They become defensive and draw a hard line between friend and foe.

Unhealthy:

Level 7
Panic-stricken
When their plans fail, or they risk losing assets that make them feel secure, they start to panic and can become volatile.

Level 8
Persecuted
They become paranoid and feel like life is out to get them. Many times, they may act out in a way that becomes a self-fulfilling prophecy – especially in relationships.

Level 9
Hysterical
They start to seek an escape route from the punishment of life. They may bring on self-inflicted injuries or contemplate suicide in severe cases. (Please seek a professional if you or someone you know is at this stage.)

Chapter 8 - Type Seven – The Enthusiast

Sevens are spontaneous and versatile. They can be seen as a busy-body. However, they can also be acquisitive and scattered. They thrive on variety.

Sevens are extroverted and optimistic. They are playful and high-spirited but still practical. They are always seeking new, exciting experiences. Sevens are always scared they're going to "miss out" on having fun or be deprived of their basic needs. Sevens crave a comfortable and sometimes lavish lifestyle.

To many, they seem undisciplined because they seem to over-extend themselves to many interests. Some of these interests are not always well-matched with their true talents.

While they seem to be scattered, many of their best ideas have been by impulse. Their "scattered" way of thinking also help them synthesize information and brainstorm ideas and solutions.

Their special abilities also equip them to learn new skills and absorb information more quickly than others. However, this is a double-edged sword because they are free to explore multiple interests and can be indecisive in their endeavors.
Sevens can be bold, pursuing life with curiosity and determination.

At their best, they have the ability to put extraordinary focus energy into their goals.

On a deeper level, you will find that Sevens share a common anxiety with Fives and Sixes. They fear they will not find satisfaction and comfort in life, which is why they bury this fear by pursuing multiple interests. They fear missing out if they don't try everything.

The consequence of their pursuits can be diminished health, strained relationships, and financial problems.

When they are well-balanced, their joy and enthusiasm become contagious to those around them.

Sevens with a Six-wing are considered "The Entertainer," while Sevens with an Eight-wing are considered "The Realist."

Stress Point
When Type Sevens are stressed, they may exhibit negative or unhealthy levels of development typically seen in Type One personalities.

These unhealthy traits include:

- Idealist
- Advocative
- Puritanical
- Judgmental
- Perfectionistic
- Dogmatic
- Intolerant
- Hypocrite
- Punitive

Security Point
During times of growth Type Sevens may exhibit positive or healthy levels of development typically seen in Type Five personalities.

These healthy traits include:

- Visionary
- Observers
- Skillful
- Independent
- Focused
- Curious

Levels of Development

Healthy:

Level 1
Full of life
Sevens take in the full experience of life. They are awed and enjoy the little things in life.

Level 2
Vivacious
Sevens in this stage are extroverts. They appreciate the little things in life and are easily stimulated.

Level 3
Multi-talented
Sevens are practical and productive. They have many talents they enjoy developing.

Average:

Level 4
Adventurous
Sevens need to stay stimulated, so they don't lose focus. This level of development is adventurous and seeks out additional options and choices.

Level 5
Hyperactive
They have a problem saying no to new responsibilities and opportunities. Instead, they throw themselves at many different adventures and are constantly active.

Level 6
Materialistic
These Sevens feel as if they never have enough. They are self-centered and always want more.

Unhealthy:

Level 7
Impulsive
They don't know how to stop giving in to their addictions.

Level 8
Mania
These Sevens have a frequent mood swing and seem to be out of control.

Level 9
Bipolar
By this point, their health and energy are depleted. They give up on themselves and life, succumbing to deep depression.

Chapter 9 - Type Eight – The Challenger

Eights perceive themselves as powerful and dominating. Their self-confidence and decisiveness are typically expressed through confrontation.

Type Eights are strong and assertive. Eights are protective and resourceful, but many times they express themselves by being ego-centric and domineering.

Eights feel as though they must gain control of their environment, including the people around them. They do not let other people's opinions sway their actions.
Eights tend to have more willpower and vitality to push through challenges and achieve remarkable results. In addition to their willpower, they also have an incredible physical strength and can endure more physical pain than other people. However, they are terrified of emotional pain. They put on a facade of strength and power to protect their feelings and avoid rejection. They would rather reject others before they can be rejected.

Eights struggle to keep their temper in check. While they create a hardcore persona, deep down they struggle with becoming vulnerable.

Healthy Eights can become masters of their strength and direct their power for good to help others. They know how to challenge others so they can grow.

Eights with a Seven-wing are known as "The Maverick," while Eights with a Nine-wing are known as "The Bear."

Stress Point
When Type Eights are stressed, they may exhibit negative or unhealthy levels of development typically seen in Type Five personalities.

These unhealthy traits include:

- Studious

- Detached
- Antagonistic
- Reclusive
- Delirious
- Schizophrenic

Security Point

During times of growth Type Eights may exhibit positive or healthy levels of development typically seen in Type Two personalities.

These healthy traits include:

- Humble
- Compassionate
- Appreciative
- Altruistic
- Empathetic
- Nurturing

Levels of Development

Healthy:

Level 1
Courageous
Eights achieve heroism and greatness by putting their interests and themselves in jeopardy for the greater good.

Level 2
Self-assertive
Eights are confident in their abilities and their opinions. They have a can-do attitude and are reluctant to back down.

Level 3
Authoritative
These people take charge and make change happen. People look up to them and trust their judgments.

Average:

Level 4
Self-sufficient
They work hard and take risks to ensure their needs are met physically and financially.

Level 5
Dominant
They want to feel as if others support them, so they boss the people around them to accept their ideas.

Level 6
Combative
They become belligerent and confrontational to intimidate others into obedience.

Unhealthy:

Level 7
Dictatorial
Their "might" makes them right. They begin to use violence to get subordinates to obey them.

Level 8
Delusional
They are delusional about how to get power and respect. They feel all-powerful like nothing can bring them down.

Level 9
Vengeful
They become dangerous to be around at their worst and attempt to destroy anything or anyone that does not conform to their will.

Chapter 10 - Type Nine – The Peacemaker

Nines are easygoing and reassuring. They can be creative and supportive to others. However, many times they become agreeable and complacent.

At their best, Nines are unshakable. They embrace the issues affecting those around them and help others work through their problems.

Nines strive for peace. Not only for others but also within themselves. They are most likely to seek guidance from the spiritual and a higher authority. The peace promised by religion appeals to their yearning for peace.

Nines may misidentify with the Intellectual (Five, Six, Seven) or Emotional (Two, Three, Four) because they don't trust their own instincts. Instead, they let their feelings sway their instincts and retreat to the depths of their mind to be comforted by mental fantasies. They encapsulate the whole of the Enneagram types. They lack a true sense of identity.

Nines attempt to emphasize the positives in life and become numb when they can't find positive solutions. They tend to minimize problems, so they are not affected by them. They need to learn how to cope with the negative and painful experiences of life.

They fear experiencing loss and separation. They believe if they can achieve peace they won't be separated from others and other people will appreciate them.
Nines with an Eight-wing are known as "The Referee," while Nines with a One-wing are known as "The Dreamer."

Stress Point
When Type Nines are stressed, they may exhibit negative or unhealthy levels of development typically seen in Type Six personalities.

These unhealthy traits include:

- Hysterical
- Feel persecuted
- Panicky
- Feel Defenseless
- Sarcastic
- Blames other people
- Evasive
- Procrastinator
- Passive-Aggressive
- Always anticipate problems
- Search for security
- Paranoid

Security Point
During times of growth Type Nine may exhibit positive or healthy levels of development typically seen in Type Three personalities.

These healthy traits include:

- Self-acceptance
- Energetic
- Ambitious
- Adaptable
- Benevolent

Levels of Development

Healthy:

Level 1
Content
They are in touch with themselves and others. They are able to form deeper and more sincere relationships with others.

Level 2
Receptive

They are emotionally strong. They easily trust others and are genuinely helpful and good-natured.

Level 3
Optimistic
They easily bring people together and are optimistic for solving problems together.

Average:

Level 4
Accommodating
They idealize the people around them. They are quick to conform to others wishes and say yes to things they don't even want to do.

Level 5
Complacent
They become indifferent toward situations and disengage emotionally from problems. Instead, they try to act as if the problem isn't even there.

Level 6
"Peace at any cost"
They appease others and neglect their own needs. They become stubborn when they feel solutions are lacking. They procrastinate and may devise "creative" solutions that do not really work.

Unhealthy:

Level 7
Repressed
They lose confidence in their ability to solve problems. Therefore, they become neglectful of others and dissociated from conflict.

Level 8
Numb
They attempt to block out anything that may stir emotion.

Level 9
Catatonic
Multiple Personality, Schizoid, and Dependent personality
disorders are possible because they abandon their true self.

Chapter 11 - How the Types Behave in Relationships

Double Type One

Both people will generally bring the same general qualities to the relationship since they share a common type. This can either be a major attraction or a potential disaster. They each have high standards they expect the other to keep. Both partners will expect important responsibilities to come first. Pleasurable activities and relationship growth will always rank low and many times become neglected.

Many times, a common interest will bring two Type Ones together. They will use the perfection of the other to help bring about a common goal. They have high expectations for the relationship as they could not handle being in a relationship with someone whose character was not stellar.

Potential Trouble

Type Ones will essentially become judgmental and intolerable of mistakes or immaturity in their partner. They are highly aware of the short-comings of both their partner and the relationship.

Instead of turning against each other, two Ones may double-team against the world. Two Ones can bring the other down to an unhealthy level of development. They may find themselves isolated from others who do not live up to their expectations.

Type One and Type Two

Type One and Type Two personalities can complement each other. Both types are interested in helping others. However, this can also become a stress point because they may focus too much attention on others, rather than their own relationship. They are very mature and independent. They fulfill their emotional needs from outside connections. They keep their relationship strong by sticking to high ideals and strong ethical standards. Many times, they use the power of two to increase their ability to help others.

This type of relationship provides elements that both types are searching for. The Type Two personality helps the Type One personality to relax. They provide nurturing and feelings the Type One desires but refuses to indulge in themselves. The Type One provides structure to the relationship, making the Type Two feel secure. The Type Two personality is generally more empathetic toward others while the Type One personality has the ideas and discernment to know what other people need.

Potential Trouble

Type Ones tend to be unaware of their needs while Type Twos become too involved serving others to tend to their needs. Therefore, both types find it hard to express their needs in the relationship. Neither type will admit they are not satisfied because both types feel striving for their own needs is selfish and forbidden. The Type One personality may resent the Type Two personality for giving too much time and attention to others instead of investing in the relationship.

The Type Two personality may feel the Type One personality is too impersonal in his/her dealings with others. Type Twos feel that while Type Ones are on a mission to improve humanity Type Twos feel like Type Ones have little to no compassion for individuals. Both types can become critical of each other.

Type One and Type Three

Both types are serious minded, idealistic, and competent. This type of relationship has the capacity to be task-oriented and driven by hard work. They both have high expectations for themselves and the relationship.

They will be more likely to actively discuss issues since neither type likes having unresolved issues in their life.

Type Ones help Threes to be more realistic and grounded. Type Threes help Ones stretch their comfort zones and encourage type Ones to not be so perfectionistic. Both types are persistent and industrious. They are concerned with excellence and efficiency and have high goals to make a real difference in the world.

Potential Trouble

The major areas of concern for this type of relationship are lack of emotional attachment, time commitments, or even a sense of competition. Ones tend to accuse Threes of being insincere in their achievements. Ones tend to feel type Three lack principle and are more concerned with the bottom-line of achieving a goal or purpose.

Type Threes generally feel Ones are inflexible and too judgmental in their attitudes. Type Threes may value the Ones' organizational ability to get things done. However, Threes often feel type Ones are too focused on the details rather than the results. Both may gradually lose respect for the other person. Type Ones lose respect for Type Threes integrity while Type Threes lose respect for Ones' effectiveness.

A break in the relationship is possible. However, it is more likely a married Type One and Type Three will keep the marriage for continued personal status.

Type One and Type Four

These two types both have a mutual interest to improve the world around them. Both are idealists. Both types can see how things could be if someone like them brought about a change to improve things.

Ones have the desire to bring truth, logical reason, and objectivity to relationships. They offer good work habits, they practice discipline and are more likely to stay and commit to relationships. Ones are diligent and focus themselves on the greater good.

Ones can become a sounding board for type Fours. They can offer advice and clarity when the Fours judgment is clouded by their feelings or self-doubt.

Fours bring to the relationship creativity, spontaneity, inspiration, sensuality, intense feelings, and the ability to tap into universal forces such as dreams or the unconscious. Their emotionality and expressiveness can provide a counterbalance to type One's formality and sense of order and reason.

Ones help type Fours bring their dreams to completion by supporting the Fours creativity with structure. Ones bring self-restraint to the relationship. This is a great model for Fours because they tend to more unregulated with their dreams and ideals.

Both types have a desire for purification and cultivation of the arts. If both partners can appreciate the strengths of each other, they can make a productive team, balancing out the limitations of each personality's limitations.

Potential Trouble

Sometimes the relationship between type Ones and type Fours is like mixing oil and water: they separate because they perceive ideas from different points of view.

Ones think they are always sensible and objective. Fours would rather see things from a personal side rather than with objectiveness.

Their idealism may not align. Ones are idealistic about external causes while Fours ideals are focused on themselves and their relationships.

Both can be condescending toward others who do not see things the same way they do. Eventually, they can turn their condescending attitude toward each other.

While both types are aware of their impulses, sensuality, and longings, they tackle the issues in opposite ways. Ones try to repress their impulses while Fours use their impulses to obtain their goals. Therefore, one of the biggest areas of conflict is self-discipline versus self-indulgence.

Ones begin to see Fours as self-absorbed and hopelessly emotional. Fours see type Ones as rigid and judgmental.

A One and Four relationship may end by being disgruntled with each other for being the way they are.

Type One and Type Five

Ones and Fives are alike in many ways. Both types repress their emotions and see themselves as fact-oriented. They both avoid letting their emotions cloud their judgment.

Ones and Fives typically enjoy each other's company because they admire each other's intelligence and expertise.

They love to laugh together at life's irrationalities. Both types highly respect personal boundaries. Neither one would make the first move unless they knew it would be appreciated by the other. Therefore, these types tend to bring formality and courtesy to each other.

Ones bring logic and order while Fives bring curiosity.

If romance develops, it develops slowly but intensely.

Potential trouble

Although both types are intellectual and alike in many ways, they can also be opposites in areas which are important to them, leading to conflict and potential break of the relationship.

Ones are concerned with objectiveness and the ultimate Truth. However, Fives do not believe in objective truth. Rather, they believe there are multiple interpretations of the Truth.

At unhealthy levels of development, Ones can become fundamentalists while Fives can become anarchist, denying the truth.

Both types have a difficult time changing their basic philosophies and lose respect for anyone who challenges their ideas. However, both types respect each other's boundaries to a fault. This can cause the relationship to become impersonal and distant.

Ones may feel type Fives are too impractical while Fives may feel type Ones are rigid, taking their opinions too seriously.

Both types can become too self-contained to contribute any energy toward the relationship.

Type One and Type Six

Type Ones and Sixes are alike in several ways to the point they are often misidentified with each other. Both types have a strong sense of duty. They are conscientious and hard workers. Both types have a desire to serve people and improve the world.

Ones bring reason and clarity to the relationship. They are confident in their actions and opinions and tend to take on the leadership role in the relationship.

Sixes offer emotional availability and bring warmth to the relationship. Their playfulness and generosity may cause type Ones to think twice about their beliefs. Sixes have more empathy to connect with people than type Ones do. Sixes take responsibility and share the burdens and chores. They are faithful and loyal to each other.

When their fundamental beliefs are aligned, these qualities can create a dynamic and highly stable team. Both types want to build a solid foundation together. Since they feel they can count on each other, it gives both people room to relax.

Potential Trouble

When there is stress in their life, Ones become all work and no play and criticize anyone who doesn't take the work as serious as they do. Too much arguing will wear down type Sixes much more than it does to type Ones.

When Sixes are stressed, they react emotionally and attempt to turn to their partner for stability. Instead, type Ones can add to the Sixes anxiety by being too critical. Sixes may create a self-fulfilling prophecy of doom to the relationship. Many times, Sixes will become defensive and evasive. They will find external activities to avoid spending time with their critical partner. They find it too difficult to talk about their anxieties in the relationship.

As type Ones become more resentful of the type Six personality, resolute Sixes will only do the minimum to contribute to the relationship. The stubbornness of type Sixes drives Ones into fits of frustration.

Resentment, anger, and even name-calling can be the result of these two personalities as the relationship deteriorates.

Type One and Type Seven

These two types are complementary opposites who can bring something needed for growth or drive the other apart by using the other's weakness against them.

Ones take pleasure in maintaining high standards. Sevens bring spontaneity and curiosity. Sevens take pleasure in fun and adventure. They don't get hung up on all the details of doing things perfectly.

One commonality between the types is they are idealistic in their plans. However, Sevens prefer having multiple options to get the job done while type Ones believe there's only one right way to accomplish their ideas. Ones believe they are keeping Sevens focused and resist distraction by having too many options. Sevens offer freedom and spontaneity while Ones make sure the job gets done efficiently.

In reality, their differences can actually support each other's goals and productivity.

Sevens offer Ones a sense of excitement while Ones bring a sense of purpose and direction. Sevens can help Ones stay lighthearted and prevent the relationship from becoming too serious.

Sevens can appreciate type One's reliability and attention to detail.

This can be a highly supportive relationship when their goals in life are aligned.

Potential Trouble

Ones will often times become too inflexible and insist things are only done their way. They see type Sevens as childish. Ones feel that Sevens are scattered and fool around too much. They feel type Sevens over-extend resources and promise too much to too many people. They believe Sevens act this way on purpose to passive-aggressively get back at the type One for some reason.

Sevens see type Ones as perfectionistic and believe they need to loosen up.

Conflicts are typically centered on organizational and financial matters. Ones feel that Sevens are reckless and wasteful. Sevens see Ones as too tight-fisted with no real vision.

Sevens will pursue other options when they feel trapped by the One's constant criticism and dissatisfaction.

Ones may lose respect for type Sevens and find them embarrassing to be around and withdraw emotional connection from Sevens.

Disdain and contempt make reconciliation difficult between these types.

Type One and Type Eight

Both types fight for truth and justice. They feel it is up to them to fix these injustices. Unfortunately, they often have different methods for fixing the problems they perceive.

They see themselves as crusaders making the world a better place. They are action-oriented and can bring about significant changes when working together for social causes. They are both perseverant and bring purpose and practicality to their missions. Both types are willing to suffer for the greater good, if necessary.

Type Eights bring a practical and immediate approach to the One's ideals.

This powerful combination can achieve results with purpose and clear personal mission. Eights provide passion that counterbalances the One's self-restraint.

Eights understand the determination of Ones and understand Ones are not easily swayed from their ideals. Eights are attracted to the challenge of getting close to Ones.

They can be opposite but can learn from each other if they are open-minded to the other's methods and values.

Potential Trouble

The differences between these types are like fire (Eights) and ice (Ones). It is easier for these types to work together rather than attempt an intimate relationship. Both types want to be in charge.

Ones may see type Eights as a rogue outlaw and may admire their bravado but abhor the chaos and destruction Ones feel it will create.

Eights often see Ones as hypocrites who preach one thing but don't keep their private behaviors in check. They see Ones as self-righteous, rigid and unrealistic about the way the world works. This may cause Eights to act out to provoke the One's judgmental nature.

Both types deny hurt and fear. Instead, they react with anger.

This type of relationship can often end with violent arguments and personal attacks on each other. This can be a difficult relationship to repair.

Type One and Type Nine

These types understand each other on a personal level because they see many of their own traits in each other.

They both bring idealism and desire for change. Both can be hard working and willing to put their own needs aside for the welfare of others.

Ones bring clarity and the ability to articulate their ideas. Nines are gentle providing nurture and support for others.

Nines prefer harmony rather than taking pleasure in being right, like a One.

Nines take away the critical and seriousness of Ones, while Ones provide clarity and direction for Nines.

This can be a highly philanthropical couple, balancing idealism with humanity.

Nines soothe Ones, while Ones remind Nines to strive for excellence.

Their love for nature, animals, and their love for their family brings them closer together.

Potential Trouble

The main conflict between these types is how they handle conflict and stress. Ones are more open about their frustration with others when things don't go their way. They obsess over who is at fault and what needs to change for improvement.

Nines are withdrawn and shut down under stress. Nines may tune out Ones and deny there's a problem. Ones will blame Nines for not taking enough responsibility to fix problems.

The more Ones push Nines to respond in a certain way, Nines become unable to succumb to Ones' ways. Nines will retreat to passive-aggressive behavior. Ones perceive the Nines behavior as resistance and negligence.

Ones lose respect for Nines and Nines become uncomfortable expressing themselves with Ones. Ones will become more self-righteous while Nines become unresponsive.

Their anger will eventually get the better of them and ultimately end the relationship.

Double Type Two

Healthy Two couples bring a high level of affection, sensitivity, and warmth to the relationship. Their genuine concern for the relationship and their partner makes them able to put a lot of energy into making sure all problems are resolved. Double Two relationships have a high level of communication. They frequently check on their partner to make sure all is well.

Healthy Twos are generous and respectful of boundaries. They understand the need for independence and individual growth while offering any resources they can to help others succeed. They express enormous affection but can also let go, creating a balance between themselves as a couple versus as individuals.

Double Twos feel secure and loyal. They know their partner will be there to help them when they need it most.

Since neither partner in a double Two relationship is accustomed to being nurtured by others, they need to learn to allow themselves to be loved and helped by the other person.

If each of the Twos can allow the support of the other, the relationship can become a source of deep love and abundance.

This can be a loving and warm-hearted couple that provides security for their family and help make the world a more loving place. This type of couple may also be open to adopting children and providing their love and nurture to those who need it most.

Potential Trouble

An intimate relationship could pose a problem for double Twos. Their need for validation from others sets them up for secret jealousy and competition for the center of attention. They may become jealous if someone chooses their partner for advice and social events.

Twos may try to charm those around them to get a reaction, which can get in the way of an exclusive intimate relationship. Some Two may begin to lose interest in their self and their looks. Others may turn to other people or food to cater to their desire for intimacy. This can cause both parties to lose physical interest in the relationship and in each other.

Unhealthy Twos are likely to develop boundary problems. They will either get overly enmeshed with each other, or one may become repulsed by their partner's hovering.

Isolation, loneliness, depression, and dealing blame can become the result of a relationship between unhealthy double Twos.

Type Two with Type Three

Most of the time both types are driven by their emotional needs. However, Type Threes are not as driven by feeling as Type Twos. Both types yearn for attention and the desire to be loved. However, type Twos are not always concerned about their own needs for attention and love.

Both types can become preoccupied with activities that put them in the spotlight among other people.

These types are sociable, charming, and high-spirited. They know how to get the attention of others while leaving a favorable impression on others around them. Each type brings energy, ambition, and the ability to communicate with people. They know how to make other people feel special like they are the center of attention.

Both people know how to recruit other people to join them on their missions and achieve goals.

Type Twos are more personal in their interactions with others. They are thoughtful and follow through with kindness and compassion.

Threes provide practicality, charm, flexibility, and goal-oriented structure for ways the couple can improve.

This type pairing can make for a special complimentary relationship. Type Twos like feeling proud of their loved ones, while type Threes strive to make their partner proud. Twos enjoy letting others be in the spotlight, while Threes enjoy being in the spotlight. Type Twos are content to be the power behind the throne, while Threes prefer to be on the throne!

As long as healthy Threes appreciate the extravagant attention from the type Two, this can be a near perfect pairing.

Potential Trouble

While some aspects of this pairing may be near perfect, every relationship has the potential for problems. This couple type has the potential to become self-conscious and even more so of their partner.

The Two personality may become jealous and possessive of Threes. They develop a feeling of "I made you – you owe me" toward the type Three. Type twos may feel unappreciated and used by type Threes. Type twos may appear as if they enjoy taking a back seat to the threes success. However, they secretly want to be recognized and feel important, but they refuse to verbally admit it. This is difficult because Threes find it difficult to thank others and share the glory. Additionally, Threes feel that Twos attempt to take too much credit for contributions.

Type Twos may undermine the Three's confidence in an attempt to feel needed by the Three. Instead, Threes distance themselves from their partner if they feel humiliation or criticism. This creates additional manipulation and anxiety for the Two.

Both types have a tendency to feel shame and vulnerability. They exploit and attempt to take advantage of their partner's weaknesses.

Both types have a hard time admitting or realizing what they truly want and need on a deeper level. In a relationship, they may assume they want the same things and are moving in that direction when in reality they may be drifting apart.

Type Twos feel neglected when Threes put other activities, such as their career, before their home and family. Twos feel type Threes should be more focused on internal morals, like love, instead of external values, like success and fame. Home and family are very important to Twos, and they cannot understand how anyone could put other duties before their home, family, and what "truly matters."

Threes feel smothered and manipulated by Twos. They feel stifled by the Twos constant need to be together and feel guilty for trying to provide a successful life for their family.

This couple needs to define what success in a relationship means to them in order to work things out and be successful.

Type Two with Type Four

Intimacy and openness are the first hurdles this couple will need to overcome. Once they are willing to share their feeling openly, this can be a passionate couple.

Healthy Twos and Fours seek warmth and connection and are willing to provide it to each other. This type of relationship can provide a safe haven for each party to share their intimate desires without criticism. They can be exactly what the other type needs.

Two provide the energy to be sociable which gives Fours more confidence when interacting with others. Twos are warm, considerate, encouraging, generous, thoughtful, and considerate with other. They are also willing to help and contribute however they can. They are practical and action-oriented.

Fours bring creativity, emotional honesty, and a sense of humor. They are willing to laugh at life's faults. They openly admit their own faults to themselves and their partner. Fours care about the impact things have on themselves and others. They have a way of bringing beauty and subtlety to the relationship.

Fours bring a sense of unpredictability and mystery. They also bring sensitivity to emotions and sensuality to the relationship.

Fours provide an environment that allows Twos to feel more nurtured and relaxed. Fours encourage Twos to discover their deeper needs and discover their true self, something Twos typically avoid on their own.

Twos appreciate the nuances and subtleness of Fours, and Fours will thrive when they are being appreciated.

These two types will lighten the mood with humor and appreciation of their quirks. Each person allows the other to mature emotionally. Both types help each other become more inner-directed and less concerned with external criticism.

Potential Trouble

While this seems like a potentially perfect pairing on the surface, in reality, there can be too much-unspoken demands and emotions for the relationship to be successful. While their common emotional issues may allow them to be more understanding of each other, it also sets up the potential for conflict.

Both types desire intimacy and closeness. They will cling to anyone who will accept their attention. Over time, they may become competitive with their friends and family's affections.

Type Twos often find Fours to be temperamental and moody. They feel Fours are too self-absorbed to care about the feelings and needs of others.

Fours believe Twos are not as genuine as they want people to believe. They have great disdain for their perception of Twos to bribe people for attention with the Twos helpfulness. In reality, Fours are often jealous of the Twos social skills and ability to easily get the attention the Fours really want. Fours will begin to feel overshadowed by the popularity of their partner. It can exacerbate the Fours' feelings of abandonment when their partner becomes too involved with other people.

Both partners may develop feelings of shame and worthlessness which will undermine the relationship. Both partners may feel their partner is too needy emotionally and not worth the effort to continue in the relationship.

Type Two with Type Five

These types portray striking opposites. Type Twos are a feeling type and a people person. Type Fives are a thinking type and more of a loner. They have different perspectives on what is important in both life and a relationship. Their striking differences present a unique challenge to each other.

Twos are enthralled with the challenge of trying to charm the Five. Twos will be the one to make the first move in initiating contact. Healthy Twos offer warmth, ease, and physical comfort. They want to improve the Five's style of life, even though Fives have no problem with their lifestyle. While they may not show it, Fives actually enjoy the attention and feeling that someone cares.

Fives are very loyal. They value any relationship that seems to be working because they typically find relationships too difficult to enjoy. Fives bring stability and calmness to the relationship. They have good judgment and the ability to be objective in a crisis. They do not dwell on the outcome of a situation. Instead, they are good advisors and make wise decisions.

Fives can also be good listeners and provide their undivided attention. Fives are calmer and more stable emotionally than Twos.

Two types take pride in warming up the Five. And, Fives secretly enjoy the nurture and attention they gave up on finding.

Potential Trouble

Respect for each other's boundaries is a common problem for this type of relationship. Type Twos get frustrated when Fives do not respond to them quickly. Fives are reserved and too involved in their own mental world and may not respond at all. The type Two personality will perceive this as rejection which will trigger fears of being unwanted and unloved. Twos may try even harder to break the Five's shell. This type of intrusion by the Two is detrimental to the Five.

Fives will detach emotionally and become withdrawn when they feel their sanctuary of inner peace is being threatened. Twos in the lower levels of development feel they are worthless when they aren't entangled in every aspect of the other person's life. Fives will perceive Twos as being irrational and out of control. Fives will become cynical about the practicality and value of being in a relationship. Fives may come to the conclusion relationships won't work for them.

The more distant the Five becomes, the more the Two becomes obsessed with pursuing the Five.

This chase for space and capture is a prescription for disaster and loneliness.

Type Two with Type Six

Twos and Sixes are both dutiful toward others. They take their responsibilities others very seriously. They put the needs of others ahead of their own needs.

Twos focus on fostering positive emotions and intimacy. Sixes attempt to construct a secure foundation for the couple.

They are both family types. They enjoy ensuring the welfare of their family, children, and closest friends. They are highly involved with their community and understand the strength that comes from having reliable social connections.

Sixes value the self-sacrifice and generosity of Twos. The loyalty of Twos makes them a strong contender for the position of a spouse for Sixes and a good parent for their children.

Twos admire the perseverance and hard work of Sixes. They rely on the Six's watchfulness to recognize difficulties before they become potential problems.

A relationship between Twos and Sixes typically becomes based on mutual respect for each other's steadiness. They may consider each other "the safe choice."

Potential Trouble

Lower functioning Sixes lack the confidence to be decisive when solving problems. They become anxious when they feel pressured by too many forces. When Twos attempt to help Sixes work through their anxiety, it comes across as additional orders and adds to the pressure they feel. Sixes perceive Twos as undermining them and their ability to conquer their problems.

Lower functioning Twos believe there can't be too much intimacy. They strive to feel closer to their partner. Sixes send mixed messages pushing the Two away before pulling them back in. This activates the Two's feelings of rejection, so they try to "help" even more. Sixes perceive the Two's "help" as being control and seek distance instead of closeness.

The back and forth behavior of Sixes may destroy the mutual respect the Two once had for them.

Type Two with Type Seven

Twos and Sevens can be outgoing, funny, friendly, and high-energy. They can be enjoyable company. These types want everyone to have fun and be happy. Both types appreciate the goodness in life. They look for the positive in all situations. They are spontaneous and engaging.

Twos are concerned with the welfare of others. They admire the gusto of Sevens to plunge ahead in life. Two expect every day to be an adventure with Sevens.

Sevens are high-energy and have a quick mind to devise plans quicker than they can be acted on. Sevens seem to radiate mental electricity and excitement; which Twos find intoxicating. Sevens remind Twos they cannot fully help others unless they help themselves first.

Sevens enjoy sharing abundance with others.

Twos help Sevens feel relaxed. Sevens feel Twos adequately fill the Seven's emotional and physical needs.

Both types are idealistic. However, Twos are more likely to translate this kind of impulse into altruistic action.

Together, they represent a generous and thoughtful couple. They can have a remarkably positive effect on those around them.

Potential Trouble

Twos feel they never have enough intimacy. They find ways to get closer to the Seven. Sevens become unsettled and upset by the idea of settling down. They see it as a limitation. Sevens are capable of long-term commitment but do not actively seek it.

Twos may become more intrusive and clingy toward the Seven. Sevens begin to feel trapped and lose interest in the relationship. Twos will want a deeper relationship but begin to perceive Sevens as untrustworthy and incapable of commitment. Sevens perceive Twos as manipulative and possessive.

Sevens need to be the center of attention to stay excited and energized. Other people become more of a selection of casual buddies that Sevens are not sincerely concerned about. Eventually, this causes Twos to feel used.

Twos will start to compensate in other ways either by withholding affection, overeating, or developing health problems.

The unhealthy behaviors of these types eventually lead to a deadlock with both parties hurt emotionally.

Type Two with Type Eight

Twos and Eights are more alike than they may appear to be at the beginning. Each is motion-oriented and want to have a private effect on their environment. Both can be sentimental and deeply feeling, with a tender side that is often hidden.

Both can play the roles of protector, provider, nurturer, and caretaker. Both types are likely to deny their own desires and needs. They have a tendency to overwork themselves, and they each want to be the strength of the relationships. Twos may become the emotional leader while Eights make all the practical decisions.

Each type brings vitality, passion, interpersonal and social capabilities, nobility, and generosity. The basic emphasis of each type is distinctly extraordinary. However, with Twos being more concerned with the welfare of others, while Eights are more concerned with the physical well-being and having a noticeable effect on their world.

They may take on roles that the opposite wants and needs: the Eight is practical and achieves results, while Twos are greater social and more philanthropical. They are both strongminded and like assuming responsibility, as long as they select it themselves. Eights soak up the adoration and affection of Twos. Two appreciate the Eight's power and efforts. Two can see through the Eight's domination and see their frequently hidden self-sacrifice.

Both types see each other's noble characteristics and may be each other's loyal supporters and admirers. Their roles also are clearly defined, so they do not get in each other's way.

Twos and Eights are exceptional at keeping each other and their relationship well-balanced. These features make them powerful allies who complement each other's strengths, especially the good effects they have on others.

Potential Trouble

Twos and Eights clearly have different values. Twos tend to be social while Eights tend to be practical. Their relationship styles are also different. Twos are empathic and indirect. Eights are independent and direct. Even Eights with an average level of development are proud of their unsentimental way of dealing with situations and people. Twos can become too attached to people and oversolicitous about their needs.

Eights are concerned with their own self-interests, while Twos are concerned with other people's interests. Eights see people as weak if they cannot take care of themselves. This can cause significant conflict over the importance of other people, including family, in the relationship.

Both types seem to have opposing views and move in opposite directions, especially concerning the treatment of others. Eights are callous and confrontational, while Twos are self-sacrificial and possessive. Their conflicts are centered around who's methods are the best. Twos will feel as if they have to apologize for their partner's behavior.

Lost respect will spell the end of the relationship between these types.

Type Two with Type Nine

Twos and Nines are very similar in their ideals. Both types are concerned with other people. They both want to create peace and help those around them.

Both types can find positives from experiences and see the positive in others. Both types are easy-going, friendly, hospitable, undemanding, and welcoming toward others.

Twos are more extroverted than Nines. Twos like to get down to details with people. Nines are more steady and quiet. They are more likely to get direct to the point than Twos. Nines have a way calming others and providing unquestioned acceptance.

Both types are attracted by each other's soothing support. Their home, pets, and environment are important to them. They go out of their way to be considerate of others.

Their best communication is through physical closeness. They can develop nearly psychic communication with each other. They are a very mellow couple. Their hospitality is healing to themselves and to others.

Potential Trouble

Both types are used to giving up their power to others. However, for a successful relationship, it's essential to have a leader. Negotiating power can be stressful for both types. Neither one wants to be the "bad guy."

Neither type is comfortable talking about how they feel. The type Two partner may step into the "boss" role but it usually doesn't fit well with them, and they may become too controlling.

Nines struggle with speaking up for themselves, but when they do, Twos will feel threatened and offended. Twos do not accept criticism well. Since Nines don't typically speak up and feel like their feelings are heard, they may go overboard with resentments that continue to build up. Nines will withdraw and become passive-aggressive to deal with their frustration.

The couple seems like they have everything together on the outside while deep down they have drifted apart. Nobody wants to accept responsibility or talk about the failure of the relationship.

Double Threes

Double Threes are concerned with achievement and excellence. They are hard workers and always want to improve their status in life and share their rewards with others.

Threes are charmers and charm their way into people's lives. Some Threes may be less sociable and more concerned with financial security.

Threes are known for the longevity of their relationships and their closeness and devotion to others.

Two Threes can form a very effective team capable of success no matter what they pursue. They are able to coordinate tasks to increase their effectiveness as a team. They want their partner to be proud of them.

Threes prefer to avoid drama and try to give their partner space to develop their own interests. Double Threes motivate each other to aim higher in their goals and achievements.

All they expect in return is respect and acknowledgment of their personal achievements.

Potential Trouble

Healthy Threes are highly supportive of each other. Problems arise at lower levels of development. Threes are known to become competitive and try to one-up their partner. Their jealousy and competition can undermine the generosity and pride they had for their partner.

It is common for Threes to compare their income and their success at work. They may use their personal successes to make their partner feel inferior.

Threes who may not have had serious relationships in the past may blame their partner for taking them away from their work. When they both focus their attention on work, they may neglect their pets, children, family, and friends.

Threes have been so accustomed to burying themselves in work that they neglect their emotional and personal needs. They may not what they truly want in life (besides success).

Eventually, their competition to be the best in the relationship leads to isolation and depression, causing the relationship to drift apart.

Type Three with Type Four

This can be a complementary relation. Each type brings important qualities the other lacks. Fours can teach Threes how to communicate on a deeper level and learn to process their feelings. They also bring sensitivity, a sense of beauty, and a feeling for fulfilling but non-practical aspects of life. Fours may help Threes increase their self-awareness and find their heart's desire. Fours also have a sense of style and refinement. They can bring rich communication to the relationship.

Threes have many of the qualities Fours desire for themselves. Threes are well-suited to share their achievements and help Fours develop new skills. Threes have tact when it comes to communicating with Fours, which can be crucial to building trust. Threes can bring a sense of ambition and practicality to the relationship. They can coach Fours through their slumps and lack of energy. They can also coach Fours on practical and professional matters as well.

Both Threes and Fours are in the feeling center of the Enneagram which can create an intense and passionate pairing. They may experience a connection that goes beyond words and reason.

Potential Trouble

Both types have issues with self-esteem. They both need validation and attention from others. They each question their identity, hiding feelings of worthlessness and shame. They often try to compare themselves and may open up competitiveness between each other. The extent of their competitiveness will depend on how much they vie for personal approval, recognition, and attention.

Threes and Fours both need to feel appreciated. Threes may seek it more openly than Fours. Fours may feel overshadowed by their partner's cry for attention. Fours may begin to feel lacking and defective.

Fours will typically devote more attention to the relationship than Threes. Fours desire more emotional intimacy than Threes are willing to provide.

Another crucial problem is both types idealize their partner for who they want them to be rather than who they really are. Fours need a rescuer and someone who embodies the qualities they lack personally. Threes see Fours as an exotic trophy to enhance their image and status to others. Both types are prone to hostility when their emotional needs are not met.

If there is no respect and admiration for each other, they will begin to undermine and dismiss each other.

Toward the end of the relationship, these types become sarcastic and snippy to each other. They begin complaining about their partner's faults to their friends.

After the relationship ends, they may try to sabotage the other out of revenge.

Type Three with Type Five

This a common, but unexpected, pairing. Fives give Threes intellectual depth. They spark creativity within Threes. Threes give Fives the professional skills they need such as confidence and how to communicate more effectively.

Both types are focused on objective issues and their work. They are preoccupied with being competent and effective. They tend to put their work ahead of their feelings.

They understand the balance between personal space and closeness, so they don't crowd each other.

Threes have unique social skills. They use charm, practicality, and energy to sell their ideas to others. They can anticipate the skills needed to achieve success, both personally and professionally.

Fives bringer deeper understanding and the perseverance to collect all the details needed to accomplish a goal.

Together, the couple can be competent, successful, and well respected. They can be a trophy for their partner depending on their attractive strengths. They both see their partner as someone who can enhance their social status.

Potential Trouble

The emphasis on work and competency shared by this couple may ultimately lead to jealousy and competitiveness. They value their self-worth based on their work and how others perceive them professionally.

Threes and Fives who work together on a project may have a different opinion on who the hero is for devising the plan. Threes want to show off their professional achievements while Fives want to show off their intellectual competency. It is common for these types to compare and even criticize each other's work.

They may argue about the efficiency (or lack thereof) of time and resources used to complete a project. They may devalue each other's priorities.

Threes can become impatient with the Fives lack of action and steps of preparation for a project. Fives may lose respect for Threes, accusing Threes of cutting corners and not as ethical.

These types are reluctant to discuss their feeling and uncertainties about their relationship until it's too late. When they do communicate, their communication is ineffectual. Fives can be too argumentative and blunt. Threes will retaliate with sarcasm and criticism. Both types may be impatient and arrogant with each other.

They begin to lose respect for each other. Fives may see Threes as dishonest and shallow. Threes may see Fives as strange and repulsive.

Turning the relationship around will depend on their shared values and how valuable they see their partner to their status and needs. Otherwise, it is near impossible to restore the relationship once their connection is broken because both types are cynical and suspicious about people.

Type Three with Type Six

This pairing is not as common as it should be. Threes and Sixes work well together as a team.

Threes bring hard work, energy, optimism, and a desire to communicate with people. They are confident in their potential to succeed, individually and as a couple.

Common goals typically bring Threes and Sixes together. They both value tangible achievements.

Sixes are more grounded. They are industrious, perseverance, and loyalty. Sixes provide support, warmth, and practicality. Sixes also have compassion for others. Threes may learn to open up and become more compassionate after being around a Six.

Both types foster mutual respect and equality for the other's special talents and interests. Threes encourage Six in their confidence. Sixes offer support without smothering Threes. Sixes may encourage Threes to become a part of something bigger and think about more than just themselves.

Their heart-centered values and principles keep them grounded, establishing a potentially successful relationship.

Potential Trouble

Despite possessing the qualities each other needs, they can also bring out the worst qualities if they are in unhealthy levels of development. They tend to have similar negative qualities in common since type Three is a stress point for type Six.

Both types can be workaholic and competitive. They look to others for reassurance. They both want to be accepted and recognized socially. Both can be a type of conformist. Threes conform to other's ideas for success, while Sixes conform to the will of those around them.

They both put their own feelings aside to achieve success. Their coping styles aggravate each other because they remind each other of their weak spots. Threes try to prove they're better than the Six. Sixes can become nervous and explode like a loose cannon on Threes. Sixes tend to be too cautious, while Threes are too ambitious.

At their worst, both types and become dishonest and shady about their actions and feelings. They may develop a relationship that has become more robotic when they ignore their feelings.

Threes will attempt to keep appearances socially and become embarrassed when the Six reveal problems between them to outsiders. They eventually lose enthusiasm and interest in each other.

Type Three with Type Seven

Threes and Sevens are a complementary pair. They both have high energy. Both types are self-assertive, optimistic, future-oriented, and outgoing. Threes and Sixes have confidence in their ability to renew relationships and professional endeavors.

Threes can work independently better than Sevens, even though both are excellent communicators and stimulate by being around others. Threes and Sevens are articulate and persuasive. Other people are attracted to them for their high energy.

No other pairing has the capability to be as gregarious and vivacious as a Three and Seven couple. They put all of their energy and heart in a variety of activities and projects, with hopes of sustaining a comfortable lifestyle for their family.

As a couple, Threes and Sevens focus on having adventures together, going on social outings, realizing possibilities and finding their full potential.

Threes bring communication skills, empathy, decorum, and appropriateness. They focus on and achieve their goals.

Sevens bring fun, resilience, spontaneity, and adventure. They are not overly concerned with failure, like Threes. Sevens bring vast knowledge and experience coupled with enthusiasm and good spirits.

Threes focus on goals, healthy limits, practicality, and the ability to stay grounded.

Threes and Sevens may seem like a magical pairing to others.

Potential Trouble

However, all that energy and competition for success can become explosive. They want to keep up their perfect couple appearance. Keeping up with appearances is exhausting, and their similar qualities may camouflage their problems from their sight.

Threes and Sevens put tremendous pressure on themselves to appear perfect and successful.

While they attempt to be light-hearted and unconcerned, their routines and overrated values cause them to unintentionally hurt each other. Yet, they hide their hurt until it consumes them and becomes too late to face them.

Threes may become workaholic and focus on advancing their career and building prestige. This places their partner and family on a back burner. Sometimes it may seem like they forget about life outside of work.

Sevens do not focus on one career. They assume they can just move on to another opportunity when one endeavor fails. Many times, Threes become jealous of the Seven's success. Seven's undermine the Threes pursuit of the perfect career and feel used by the Three.

Threes and Sevens avoid talking about their insecurities for as long as possible (sometimes too long). It often takes a crisis for their problems to surface.

Neither one wants to be in a monotonous and failed relationship. So, they shift their focus to self-centered interests until the relationship comes to a permanent end.

Type Three with Type Eight

Threes and Eights can form powerful, passionate, highly effective, and stimulating relationships. They are both assertive and fight for what they want in life. Both types tend to stand out in their social cliques. When brought together, it is inevitable they will notice each other.

Threes and Eights will either form a formidable alliance or become fierce competitors. The Eights strength actually gives Threes the ability to be more sensitive. Eights feel reliable, and Threes need security before they can open up. Eights enjoy watching Threes take charge and overcome challenges. Eights begin to relax when they understand Threes are capable of taking care of themselves.

Threes and Eights are pragmatic, action-oriented, and they make sure the job gets done even if they have to take control to achieve their goals. They are both persuasive and self-confident. They are not afraid to cut their losses when things don't work out.

Threes are more aware of public relations, and they know how to please people. They are adaptable and diplomatic.

Eights bring directness, physical vigor, fearlessness, and determination to achieve their personal vision. They offer decisiveness, solidity, and strength. Threes gain confidence from the Eight.

Threes and Eights want to support each other and be proud of each other's accomplishments and potential. They usually direct their competitiveness towards other people.

Potential Trouble

This type of pairing is better off in the business world when energy, determination, and drive are crucial to success. Both types are workaholics. They put tremendous pressure on themselves to achieve goals and be successful.

Under stress, their personal success may become more important than their relationship. In this case, they will attempt to compete with their partner, rather than support them.

Eights are more open about how controlling they are. Threes use manipulation and subtlety to control others, which can make Eights suspicious and lose respect and trust for Threes. After they lose trust, Eights become jealous and possessive. They order their partner to do things to prove loyalty. Threes may feel used and belittled when they don't have appreciation for their partner.

Eights will begin to demand loyalty until Threes feel like they can no longer pursue their own goals. Eights see the Three as untrustworthy and deceitful. Threes may see the Eight as vengeful and willful.

Both types become manipulative to get their way. They will lose each other's trust completely. Threes and Eights lack the ability to express their feelings for fear of becoming vulnerable. Suspicion and isolation become their normal and is difficult to break.

Threes and Eights battle for leadership and who supports who in the relationship.

Type Three with Type Nine

Threes can feel supported with a Nine beside them. Nines bring encouragement, support, and pride in the Three's accomplishments.

Threes are able to explore their potential and be the best version of themselves. Threes also help Nines to have more self-respect and learn to invest in themselves.

Nines help Threes find enjoyment and relax in simple things. They give Threes permission to not overwork themselves.

Both types avoid conflict and always find positivity. Nines genuinely look on the bright side with optimism. Threes focus on keeping a hopeful and positive attitude. Threes make sure no one sees them depressed or having a rough time.

Threes and Nines are idealistic and sociable. They care for children, animals, and the underdog. Nines and Threes are hardworking. They want material success to enable them to take care of others. They want an aesthetically pleasing home.

Threes bring ambition, energy, flexibility, goal management, and efficiency. They energize Nines and bring excitement and change to the relationship.

Nines bring steadiness, nonjudgment, and security. Nines assure Threes they are loved for being themselves and not just for achievements.

Potential Trouble

This kind of relationship may be "too much of a good thing." Both types are attracted to keeping life positive.

Nine may be able to provide for the materialistic needs of the relationship but can become emotionally absent. Threes become depressed when they fear being rejected or abandoned.

Threes may feel their success is stifled by the Nine. Nines may feel like the Three is spoiled and too demanding.

Threes and Nines are reluctant to bring up complaints. They don't want to disrupt their relationship with negative energy.

Threes are scared to complain about fear of rejection. Nines feel it is better to let things work itself out without disturbing the peace.

It often takes an affair, crisis, or other major challenge to reveal the true state of the relationship. Threes and Nines are more likely to go through cycles of being "On-and-off." However, they won't have a successful relationship until the underlying problems are dealt with.

Double Fours

Double Fours make good friends. Typically, they feel misunderstood by other personality types. However, with other Fours, they share a sense of understanding.

Fours can be more open with each other. They may share their deepest, darkest secrets, their childhood experiences, their dreams, and even their disappointments. They are also open and sensitive to the needs of others. They expect the same sensitivity and openness in return, and they can find it in other Fours.

They treat their relationship as a safe haven where they can be open and honest. Their fear of being too different is relieved when they are with each other.

Potential Trouble

Emotional instability is the primary concern when dealing with Fours. They can be self-absorbed and point out all the faults in the relationship. They want their personal emotional issues to be the center of attention. Each person wants to feel special and be treated with "kid gloves" so to speak. However, they may resent their partner for wanting the same treatment. They both want someone who will rescue them from themselves.

Fours have significant lack of trust in others. Therefore, they tend to withdraw from conflict and confrontation. Fours may try to test their partner beyond what they can handle. They become intolerant until they begin to tread softly around their partner, never really dealing with significant issues in the relationship.

Four may become moody and passive-aggressive with the one person they were so in love with. Their arguments and rejections will eventually damage the relationship past the point of no return.

Type Four with Type Five

Fours and Fives bring rich qualities of aspects of human development. Fours have an artistic and emotional temperament. Their habit of introspection enables them to be sensitive to their own feelings and other's feelings.

Both types are private but enjoy deep conversations and experiences. They appreciate each other's differences. They respect each other's commitment to follow their interests.

Fives are inquiring and intellectual. They have a habit of asking questions and exploring vast interests.

Fours appreciate the effect new discoveries have on people. They understand the significance of the Fives intellect to bring about enlightenment to the relationship and to others.

Both types are creative, and they love the stimulation of sharing their discoveries with each other. They are sincerely interested in listening to their partner. Both types enjoy humor and talking about bizarre and outlandish news. Their relationship may be described as quirky, unique, and full of character.

Fives introduce Fours to new worlds and new perspectives. Fours help Fives get in tune with their feelings. They inspire creativity in each other and encourage each other to be themselves.

Potential Trouble

Intimacy versus personal space is the greatest conflict for Fours and Fives.

Fives tend to be more private and not ready for intimacy. Fours feel Fives are too intellectual to sympathize with their emotional needs. They feel Fives are too impractical and take too long to take action.

Fives feel drained by the Four's emotional needs. Fives feel Fours are too wrapped up in their feelings to be rational and can be unstable.

Fours get frustrated with the superficial attention (they feel) they get from Fives.

Unless Fives can learn to appreciate the Fours deep feelings, and Fours can learn to appreciate the Fives minimal emotions and boundaries, this type of relationship may not work out.

Type Four with Type Six

Fours and Sixes have natural attractions for each other because they are both emotional and insecure with themselves around people. Both let their intuition and feelings guide their decisions.

Sixes may actually misidentify as Fours due to the qualities they have in common. These similar qualities may even be the attraction bringing this couple together. Their commonalities create empathy and tolerance for each other. They may consider each other kindred souls. They understand each other's distrust of others and fear of abandonment.

Fours and Sixes tend to support each other by allowing each other to vent their complaints and worries they would not feel comfortable discussing with others.

Fours bring sensuality, sensitivity, and the ability to express emotion. Fours can teach Sixes how to express some of their emotions and how to talk about their personal issues.

Sixes bring hard work, practicality, perseverance, and loyalty. They also express concern about the security of their relationship. Sixes are also warm and playful and may be able to brighten the Four's spirit. Sixes enjoy practicality. They give Fours space to develop their creativity. Sixes give Fours support and time to work through emotional issues.

Fours make Sixes feel needed, increasing the Sixes confidence.

A relationship between Fours and Sixes can fill in the gaps and help each other seek higher levels of development.

Potential Trouble

Their feelings of abandonment typically lead to problems in this type of relationship. Unhealthy Fours and Sixes may be pessimistic, critical, and become emotionally reactive, feeling overwhelmed. They will test each other's loyalty. They may prepare for the end by withdrawing their affection. However, many times, this creates a self-fulfilling prophecy.

Fours and Sixes may become codependent. However, this type of codependency usually does not result in personal growth. Instead, it creates unhealthy dependency connected with a lower self-esteem – that they are nothing without the other.

Fours may welcome change by being interested in improving themselves as a person. They can also welcome adventure. However, Sixes are resistant to change. Many times, Fours will perceive the Six is trying to hold them back.

Fours and Sixes can be self-doubting and pessimistic. They are mistrustful of others around them.

Fours desire more romance and free-spirit from Sixes. Sixes desire more dependability from Fours.

In this type of relationship, problems and conflicts escalate quickly, leading to massive over-reactions.

Type Four with Type Seven

Fours and Sevens are intrigued by each other, representing a typical case of opposites attracting.

Fours are introverted, quiet, self-doubting, pessimistic, and emotional. Sevens are extroverted, outgoing, self-confident, intellectual, and optimistic.

Sevens may help Fours overcome their shyness and their reluctance to try new experiences.

Fours respect the Seven's feelings and keep Sevens focused on their true desires.

Together, they highlight the contrast of their differences. They think differently. They react and find pleasure in different ways. They find their differences fascinating and intriguing.

Fours and Sevens invite ecstasy and joy, spontaneity, passion, and emotion. Fours and Sevens can be irreverent, but funny and entertaining.

They enjoy rich conversation and can pass hours communicating their thoughts, reactions, and even the mundane details of their life. They desire the finer things life has to offer – lavish food and wine, top of the line clothes and household furnishings, and travel. Many times, they overspend to accommodate their lifestyle. Fours and Sevens desire the latest and greatest. A dash of romance and adventure will keep their relationship fresh and lively. Their seemingly perfect lifestyle is an inspiration and joy to others.

Opposites such as Fours and Sevens are likely to balance each other. Fours are deep and inward. Sevens are fun and extroverted.

Potential Trouble

There must be a strong force early in the relationship to keep these two types together. Otherwise, the relationship will fall apart quickly. Fours and Sevens are impulsive and easily frustrated with others when things don't go as planned. They have high expectations for the quality of attention they receive from others.

If they are not upfront about their complaints, neither type will give each other many chances to make up. Fours envy and admire the Seven's high energy and resilience. However, they wear down quick by the Seven's fast-paced lifestyle. Fours perceive Sevens as insensitive and superficial.

Sevens may try to imitate the Four's creativity and appreciation of beauty. However, they also perceive Fours as impractical and ineffectual.

When the quality of the relationship worsens, Fours become hostile. Sevens become impatient and verbally abusive. Fours will want to talk things out. Sevens are quick to move on. By the end of the relationship, their cute quirks become irritating and insufferable to each other.

Type Four with Type Eight

This relationship will either be uniquely creative or innately volatile. Fours and Eights have strong emotional responses. They both act to get a reaction from their partner. They are both dominating. Eights are dominant in their interactions with people. Fours are dominant with their emotions.

Fours and Eights bring intensity, passion, deep (unconscious) feelings, and energy to all parts of the relationship. They are attracted to each other's hidden qualities, vulnerability, and even each other's storminess. Both types understand neither person are what they seem on the surface.

Fours and Eights are highly intuitive. Fours are knowledgeable and self-aware of their feelings. Eights are intuitive about external occurrences.

Their (Four and Eight) passions can cause them to become reckless and impulsive, which can be exciting. However, with all exciting impulses, there's usually a trade-off. Fours depend on the practicality of Eights for provision and protection. Eights depend on the challenge of getting inside the Four's emotional world.

Fours see charisma, strength, and solidity in Eights. Fours and Eights challenge themselves to live up to the other person's level of intensity. They make each other feel alive. Vitality, intensity, immediacy, and passion are the emotional hallmarks of a relationship between these types.

Potential Trouble

Fours and Eights take pride in being seen as larger-than-life. Eight's quest for control and willpower make them seem larger-than-life. Fours quest for self-expression and their strong connection to feelings make them seem larger-than-life.

Fours and Eights want to be free from control. They become quickly enraged if they feel pressured by someone's control. They are both prone to depression, rage, and vengeance.

Arguments and fighting become common in their relationship. They will withdraw affection and verbally condemn each other to "teach each other a lesson," many times in public to inflict shame and embarrassment.

Their relationship can become a heated passion. Fours and Eights also enjoy the process of fighting just to make up. They find their relationship more exciting.

Many times, they will drag outside family into their squabbles and make them choose sides.

Type Four with Type Nine

Fours and Nines are private and withdrawn. They can also be sensitive to the needs and feeling of others. Both types are empathetic to those who are suffering.

Fours and Nines are idealistic in search of their perfect soulmate. They desire a deep connection, but also want a sense of privacy. They are both highly creative, and they support each other in their creative endeavors. They are willing to give each other the space they need to foster their talents.

Their lifestyle likely expresses their sensuality and desire to be comfortable in life. Fours and Nines are comfortable staying home and enjoying each other's company. They bring appreciation and passion for each other.

Fours can help Nines express their feelings. Nines help Fours feel accepted and understood as a person. Fours are good at deciphering feelings. Nines will appreciate the Four's emotional storms and drama.

The passion this couple has for each other is in the understanding of their emotions on a deeper level.

Potential Trouble

As with everyone, Fours and Nines react differently to stress. Fours are demanding and emotionally volatile. Nines become disengaged.

Nines abhor the Four's sense of entitlement. Fours despise the Nine's irresponsibility of not learning from their experiences.

Nines will continue to shut down until communication is nonexistent. They don't want to hear about the Four's reactions or feelings. Fours see the relationship as ineffectual and boring. They start to feel contempt toward their partner and the relationship.

Fours and Nines seek partners who have strengths in the qualities they lack themselves. In unhealthy relationships between these types, their desires are not met, and they become stuck in the chaos of anger, irritation, and resentment with each other.

Double Fives

Another Five seems like the perfect soulmate for this type. Fives stimulate their minds and are well informed. They are imaginative, independent, fact-oriented, and non-intrusive. Their idea of a perfect date night includes a good debate and a good movie.

Fives don't want to be controlled. Double Five relationships may be characterized by courtesy, respect for boundaries, and no expectations.

They don't like people knowing their personal details. They can provide each other with the space they need. They would never put someone on the spot for personal information or make personal demands. They may be curious about others, but they have a hard time opening up and trying to get others to open up.

Fives must learn to balance independence, intimacy, and sharing personal matter for the relationship to be successful. Once Fives find someone they feel comfortable with, they can become attached quickly. However, they may not be open about it right away, until they feel sure they won't be rejected.

Their communication is many times more intellectual than verbal.

Potential Trouble

Double Five relationships may become too intellectual. Fives may try to over analyze their partner, rather than try to identify with them.

They may try to designate strong boundaries and become secretive about their personal life and intentions.

They may also get into heated arguments over trivial matters. Each person feels their ideas and way of thinking is right. When in fact, the matter is so trivial they may both be right, and it probably doesn't matter as much as they think.

The emotional distance they put between them and their partner is typically the ultimate conflict in their relationship. They become too isolated from each other. They may even withdraw from the world around them as well.

Type Five with Type Six

Fives and Sixes are intellectual types with significant differences. They have respect for the intellectual insight, technical mastery, and expertise of their partner. They are likely to begin their journey as colleagues before gradually developing into an intimate relationship over time.

Fives and Sixes respect attention to detail and accuracy, craftsmanship, and the skills to analyze situations without bias. Together, they can be effective in handling crises situations. They are watchful for potential problems and draw from their personal experience and expertise.

Fives offer detached objectivity, penetrating curiosity, and an unwillingness to settle for an answer without thoroughly testing it. Sixes bring high ideals and values that make them less objective but inject a sense of humanity.

Sixes lack the self-confidence to make decisions. Therefore, they turn to experts for advice. Fives are skeptical of authority and rely on their own intuition.

The devotion and care of Sixes can break through and open up Fives who have a tendency to isolate themselves.

There must be unwavering trust for this type of pairing to work.

Potential Trouble

Fives and Sixes think and work in diametrically opposite ways. There will be plenty of emotional and intellectual tension between them.

If the trust and communication between Fives and Sixes deteriorate, Fives begin to see Sixes as indecisive and too conventional. Sixes are then afraid to make a mistake within sight of their partner for fear of criticism and rejection.

Sixes may seem prejudicial, close-minded, political and petty, and appeasers of authority rather than a seeker of truth. Five seem unwilling and unable to work as a team. Sixes perceive the Five's ideas and methods as impractical and a waste of time.

They each contribute to each other's sense of hopelessness and powerlessness.

Without intentional hard work at building a solid relationship, these types may be better off as friends.

Type Five with Type Seven

Fives and Sevens bring a lot of intellectual energy and appreciation of ideas to a relationship. Each party brings qualities the other person is lacking.

Fives bring clarity, depth, insight, self-reliance, independence, and a whimsical sense of humor. They love knowledge and intellectual pursuits and have quick minds.

Sevens bring quickness of spirit. They are ready for anything at the drop of a hat. Sevens enjoy being dependent but may also choose select friends to celebrate their adventures with. They are extravagant, generous, outgoing, gregarious, and the life of the party.

Fives tend to be more frugal with resources and money. They are private until you get to know them and they feel more secure. Fives keep Sevens grounded, and they encourage them to stick with their endeavors long enough to see if they will pay off. Sevens encourage Fives to come out of their shell and meet new people and try new experiences.

Fives and Sevens enjoy communication and exploring new places together. Their differences can balance each other out.

Potential Trouble

Fives minimize their expectations of life, especially during stress. They perceive the world as lacking experts to meet the demands of this world. Fives detach and withdraw emotionally. They become even more isolated and reclusive.

Sevens are accustomed to quick action and multiple back-up plans and escape routes. As pressure increases, they keep trying to do more to distract them from their anxieties.

The reactions of Sevens cause Fives to withdraw even more. They perceive Sevens as out of control, and the Five begins to fear the Seven.

In lower levels of development, Fives perceive Sevens as intrusive, superficial, and coarse. Sevens continue to try harder to get Fives to join in on their fun.

Fives are embarrassed by the Seven. And, Sevens perceive Fives as unresponsive and cold. Sevens become pushy and demanding. Fives become uncooperative and withdrawn.

Without trust to work out the difference, their differences will only get worse.

Type Five with Type Eight

Fives need to be more in-tune with their instinctive energy. They need to engage with the practical world and accept their own sense of power.

Eights need to be more aware of the impact their actions have on themselves and their environment. They need to consider the consequences before they act.

Fives and Eights insist on independence. They are aware of boundaries and despise intrusion. Fives and Eights enjoy debate and appreciate someone with strong character. They feel like outcasts and can understand each other on a deeper level.

Despite their need for space, Fives and Eight may discover their vulnerabilities and sense of need for their partner. Both types can be impassive their own unhappiness and suffering.

As a couple, they bring action and thoughtfulness, power and depth, brashness and brilliance to their world. Together, Fives and Eights, protect and advise each other.

Potential Trouble

Five are indifferent to the physical and practical goals Eights have. Fives feel valuable to the world when they can sacrifice their personal luxuries for advancement.

Eights take pride in their worldly achievements and status. Eights use their might and energy to intimidate people and gain control.

Five shut down in response to stress. Eights become threatening and confrontational.

Fives and Eights are sensitive to rejection, and they experience the feeling of rejection easily.

Fives can lose respect for anyone they perceive as destructive and irrational. They will physically leave in order to feel safe. Eights will retaliate in any way possible. If the Eight leaves first, Fives will react to rejection with cynicism and depression.

Type Five with Type Nine

Fives and Nines offer emotional and personal space for enjoying separate activities.

They don't intrude or hover on their partner. They seem to have a healthy emotional interest in each other.

Fives and Nines are characterized by respect for each other's boundaries and individualism. Nines are uncritical and undemanding.

Despite being the more emotional between the two, Nines do not always know how to express their feelings. Nines appreciate the Five's ability to ask the right questions.

Fives appreciate the Nine's warm and nurturing qualities. Nines are able to help Fives to relax completely.

Fives and Nines may help initiate alternative worldviews for each other through their relationship.

Potential Trouble

Tensions between Fives and Nines grow due to the space they are willing to give each other. They are aware of boundaries and would not want to intrude on someone's boundaries.

Both Fives and Nines can be so out of touch with their feelings they do not know how they feel about each other.

Nines are more emotionally available, but they tend to idealize their partner, especially when they are together. Nines can get an "out of sight, out of mind perspective" regarding their partner. Generally, no one can live up to the idealizations Nines create about their partner.

Fives perceive the "out of sight, out of mind" attitude as an on/off the relationship. They become frustrated, cynical, and depressed about the relationship.

Fives and Nines can become disconnected from themselves and each other. They live in their imagination rather than reality. Solitary interests steal the Fives attention, while the pursuit of peace and more supportive relationships draw away the Nine.

Without a substantial effort to see each other frequently, the relationship between Fives and Nines will evaporate away.

Double Sixes

Strong Six couples make a point to understand each other. Two Sixes usually bond quickly, sensing a kindred spirit. Double Sixes will have shared secrets and values. They stimulate each other intellectually.

Trust is extremely important to Sixes. They can allow themselves to relax and enjoy themselves by developing a deep trust between them. Trust allows double Six couples to voice their doubts and suspicions, to test ideas, and to discover how they really feel about situations. They give each other a lot of mutual support and protection. They will rush to the other's aid without hesitation.

Loyalty and commitment reinforce the feelings of safety and security they build together. There may also be a lot of unspoken sensitivity in a double Six relationship.
Sixes are not skillful at talking about their feelings directly. They express their feelings and attitudes through their actions and through their dedication and steadfastness. They inspire each other to work towards happiness – more so than they would for themselves.

Potential Trouble
Double Six couples tend to be emotionally reactive. Once a spirit of negativity creeps in, they begin to feed off each other's fears. Double Sixes can get into worst-case scenarios and other forms of magnifying problems until they both feel like crises are everywhere and believe they are doomed. Sometimes they will act on impulse, without thinking through their situation or finding a solution to their problem. They may haphazardly take action—any action—to relieve their anxiety.

Alternatively, Double Sixes can become indecisive and fall into a stalemate and a feeling of confusion, unable to act. Since Sixes are emotionally reactive, they tend to become oversensitive and argumentative with each other. They will blame each other for the situation and for not providing a solution. They will continue to shift the blame back and forth to buy time to work through their anxiety until they reach a solution.

Double Sixes can be a very tense pairing with lots of outbursts, yelling, arguments, and blaming.

Unhealthy Sixes may be semi-hysterical and keep everyone on edge with nervous pessimism. Double Sixes have fears which are based on speculations about the future and irrational. Therefore, it be difficult to break the pattern of anxiety between the Sixes.

Double Sixes tend to wear each other out with their worrying, negativity, suspicion, and eventual mistrust of each other. This type of couple may find it near impossible to reestablish trust due to each other's accusations, feelings of betrayal, and lack of support.

Type Six with Type Seven

Sixes and Sevens are both intellectual. They can offer reinforcement of each other's strengths. In other areas, they tend to counterbalance the other person's limitations. Sevens are more entertaining and uplifting to Sixes. They are quick witted and enjoy bantering with each other. Sevens are the brainstormers while Sixes are good at implementing plans to get the job done.

Sevens are good at calming the fears of Sixes and helping Sixes move beyond their fears. Sixes bring commitment and loyalty to the Seven.

Sixes are more in touch with reality and what can be accomplished with the limitations at hand. Sevens rely on the expertise and grounded-ness of Sixes.

Sevens teach Sixes resilience and how to not fear the future while Sixes teach Sevens the difference between optimism and a pipedream.

Potential Trouble

Sixes and Sevens may complement each other's strengths when they are healthy. However, in the average to lower Levels, the picture can shift quickly. Sixes are interested in predictability and security, foreseeing problems and creating plans to prevent future problems. Sixes are aware of limitations and why things cannot be done as planned. In contrast, Sevens seek relief from their anxiety.

Sevens are interested in overcoming limitations, seeing new possibilities, and trying new things. Sevens are impatient and insensitive to problems and obstacles. Sixes tend to be pessimistic and negative, while Sevens tend to be optimistic and positive.

Sevens are concerned with the future, while Sixes tend to dwell on the past and the lessons they can learn from history to prevent things from going bad again.

Sixes desire someone who they can have a long-term commitment with. Sevens are reluctant to enter relationships requiring a long-term commitment. Sixes tend to feel that Sevens are too self-indulgent. Sixes question the loyalty of Sevens.

Sixes oppose everything. They are distrustful and get suspicious easily. Sixes live a life of self-imposed rules and limits. Sevens tend to feel that Sixes worry too much, and make themselves (and those around them) crazy by raising questions and objections about everything before trying anything new.

In this type of relationship, these two opposing viewpoints reflect the different expectations Sixes and Seven have from their partner, life, and relationships. Unless their differences can be reconciled, it will be difficult for this relationship to stand the test of time.

Type Six with Type Eight

Sixes and Eights can build an exceptionally strong and long-lasting relationship. They feel most people are selfish and can't be trusted. They believe life is highly unpredictable. Eights develop an attitude that they are the only one responsible for their happiness and must do what it takes to protect it. Sixes rely on select friendships they feel they can trust.

Both types have longstanding issues with trust and may put each other through tests to determine their loyalty. Once they have bonded they never become indifferent to each other despite any changes in the relationship.

Sixes and Eights try to embody strength and protectiveness. They both admire honesty, loyalty, hard work, responsibility, and courage. Both types enjoy fighting for the underdog.

Sixes and Eights are doers. You will never see them sitting around thinking about what needs to be done because they are already out doing it. Their goal is to create a safe and secure environment for their self and their loved ones.

Sixes desire connection and commitment. They bring sensitivity, warmth, and playfulness to the relationship.

Sixes are more intellectual. Their skepticism and analytic thinking give them the ability to think through decisions and foresee potential problems before acting. They tend to provide advisement while Eights provide the leadership and audacity Sixes lack.

Challenges and adversity energize Eights and their can-do spirit. Their strong will and confidence give them directness and decisiveness in carrying out plans.

Sixes idealize Eights as their hero, softening the Eight's hard exterior. Eights are warmed by the devotion of Sixes to them.

Eights are mindful of their inner struggles, and they know what it takes to rise above them.

While fireworks between these types may be inevitable at times, with genuine affection, the bond between them will still grow stronger over time.

Potential Trouble

Both types are emotional but don't always know how to face their emotions. Eights hide their emotions and vulnerability under a veneer of toughness and bravado. Sixes hide their emotions and vulnerability under a shell of defensiveness and bluster.

Both types become offensive and attempt to counterattack when they feel threatened.

Eights set the tone and take leadership in the relationship. They expect others to adapt to them instead of the other way around. Eights are amused by the independence of others because they see themselves as the only one capable of being in charge.

Counterphobic Sixes may seek out the leadership they fear. Most of the time, Sixes can handle and appreciate the Eight's leadership. However, there are times when they feel the need to push back and prove they are nobody's puppet. This creates a power struggle between the two types. This creates more fights and ongoing power struggle.

Anxious Sixes will attempt to avoid confrontation with Eights. Eights will sense their passive-aggressiveness and question the Six's loyalty. Eights will become condescending toward Sixes if they feel Sixes are wavering and weak in their position.

The Eight's tendency for rage only exacerbates the relationship problems. Without trust and respect, their relationship will certainly end.

Type Six with Type Nine

Sixes and Nines can be a very stable relationship. Despite their differences, deep down they desire the same things. Sixes need security and predictability while Nines need autonomy and stability.

Both types need a solid foundation they can depend on. They expect good work and honesty to be rewarded. They tend to abide by the rules and very rarely question authority. However, they can also demonstrate a rebellious (Six) or counterculture (Nine) streak, giving them a unique sense of individualism.

Sixes and Nines depend on their childhood experiences and beliefs to guide them in adulthood. They seek a partner with similar belief and values.

While they experience many similarities, they are still very different. Sixes are more skeptical and questioning of the world around them. Sixes expect people to prove themselves to them. Nines may be too trusting and sometimes naïve. Nines offer optimistic support and acceptance.

Sixes tend to spot the exceptions and focus on the complications of a situation rather than find an acceptable solution. Nines can see the overall picture and find a solution to fix the problem.

Both types have difficulty defining what makes them special as a person. However, together they can bolster each other's confidence through their harmony with each other.

Sixes and Nines with a balanced relationship may believe they have found their soulmate.

Potential Trouble

Trouble comes when they start to clam up and can't express their problems to each other. Both types can become defensive and stubborn. They want to make the other person guess what's wrong. Their stubbornness may create a stalemate between the couple.

They may develop psychological or physical health problems to guilt their partner into taking care of them.

Sixes frequently feel guilty and do whatever they can to make up and keep their position secure. Nines will meddle and manipulate people to keep them together. They go along with others despite their own stressors and problems.

Both types value familiarity and security. They avoid confrontation as long as possible. Sixes tend to have the shorter fuse and may explode on the Nine creating permanent and irreversible damage to the relationship.

Double Sevens

Sevens represent spontaneity, high energy, and interest in anything fresh and exciting. When Sevens are well balanced and healthy, there is a sense of abundance and joy that permeates their relationship and overflows to those around them. Healthy Sevens will exude happiness.

Sevens are sensitive, generous, thoughtful, and idealistic. They are sociable and provide good company for each other. They expect personal freedom and don't want to be tied down by commitments or routine. They are careful to not impose too many rules or expectations on each other.

Sevens are resilient and optimistic. They are ready to start over with a fresh perspective when they encounter difficulties.

Their relationship is guided by their gratitude for having each other.

Potential Trouble

Sevens lack the patience need to develop a relationship with a solid foundation. They want a complete and developed relationship right away. Their high expectations make it difficult to work through the growing pains of a relationship.

Sevens may seek other endeavors when the relationship is no longer stimulating and exciting. Sevens hate commitment because they always feel like they are missing out on something better. Double Seven relationships are worse because neither one wants to be the first to risk commitment and rejection.

Sevens are often impulsive and don't consider the consequence of their actions and words. They act in the heat of the moment. They tend to be insensitive toward each other in these moments.

Sevens crave constant stimulation socially. This is great if their social lives mesh but devastating when they don't. They lose interest in spending time together, and each person is determined to not get rejected by the other.

Type Seven with Type Eight

Sevens and Eights are independent, strong-willed, and self-assertive. They resist being controlled by authority, their partner, or even their own personal desires. They will respond with a defiance to push the limits.

Both types look for practical, concrete results. They want the harvest of their actions immediately and refuse to sacrifice present happiness for promises of happiness in the future.

Both types are prone to overspending because they want to lavish others with their money as a symbol of their success.

Both types have exceptional energy, vitality, and gusto for life. They achieve results and stay active. Both are willing to try new things and have a sense of adventure.

Both types are outspoken with their opinions and their needs.

Sevens keep their communication light and fun. They are highly engaging storytellers and conversationalists. They turn both their troubles and adventures into entertaining tales.

Eights are more reserved and moody. They need Sevens to lighten their environment and keep their affairs more enjoyable.

Eights bring directness and face difficulty with persistence and determination.

Potential Trouble

Sevens and Eights need to find positive channels for their unique energy and interests. Failure to do so will result in destructive ways of releasing energy. They may their energy against each other.

Sevens and Eights are strong-willed and independent. They resist being controlled by their partner. Eights will bully and threaten Sevens when they don't get what they want. Sevens may become condescending and insulting toward Eights.

Both types will flaunt their defiance as a badge of honor. They can be extremely self-centered, making it seem as if the world must revolve around them and their desires.

Both types are addicted to the adrenaline rush of reckless behavior. Sevens and Eights verbally abuse their partner with words other people would never even allow themselves to think, much less verbalize. Fights between Sevens and Eights can turn into public scenes of verbal and physical violence.

They build their relationship to the point of no return that may end with tragic consequences.

Type Seven with Type Nine

Seven and Nine partnerships are very common because they bring a good mix of similar and opposite qualities. Sevens and Nines are both optimistic, upbeat and strive to avoid conflict and negativity.

Both types are sociable, friendly, and overall happy with themselves and their lives. Both types tend to move forward rather than dwell on problems of the past. Both partners will forgive and forget quickly. They do whatever they can to bring out the best in a situation, to build a solid foundation for their foundation.

Sevens and Nines tend to be practical but use romance and physical intimacy to spice up their relationship. They use humor to get through the mundane moments of life.

Sevens have the ability to stimulate Nines when others can't. Sevens tend to be more self-assertive than Nines. Sevens take the initiative, bring energy, and lay out plans for the relationship. Sevens are confident but curious and open to new experiences. They are resilient to setbacks. Sevens bring fun and adventure.

Nines are steadfast and supportive. They provide acceptance and tend to be more sympathetic and soft-hearted. Nines are more relaxed and less demanding.

Nines are generous and more willing to make sacrifices to keep others happy. Their simplicity meshes well with the Sevens assertiveness.

There can be a good balance between energy and relaxation if these two types don't take advantage of each other.

Potential Trouble

Sevens and Nines have difficulty working through the rough patches of life and relationships. Both prefer keeping everything positive and agreeable. They are quick to pass blame when problems arise. Neither one is willing to take responsibility for the fall of the relationship.

The angry demands of Sevens send Nines into withdrawal and inaction. They become stubborn and shut down.

Sevens are more inclined to talk about their problems with little resolve to handle the problem. Sevens tend to become verbally abusive toward the Nine.

Sevens feel Nines are indecisive and incompetent. Their criticism and contempt only push Nines further into withdrawal. Sevens justify their criticism by saying honesty demands them to express their disdain toward the Nine.

One of the most carefree couple types can become miserably strenuous if they are unable to communicate their feelings and work out their problems.

Double Type Eight

Due to the typical characteristics of type Eights, this can be one of the most explosive pairings. Few relationships will compare to the intensity between two Eights. Type Eights bring a lot of passion, vitality, and energy to the relationship.

Eights have strong willpower. They are independent in their thinking and make decisions they feel will be most effective. They want to see practical results.

Eights are quick to act on their impulses. They don't just talk about doing something, they go do it.

Eights ironically can be a perfect pair. When their levels and dominant traits are well matched, they can both stimulate and help each other relax.

They know they have met their match. Therefore, they can let down their guard and relax around each other, turning their focus to external interests.

Two Eights know what it takes to become a team and get things done while creating an environment of security and stability.

Eights are a couple that exudes confidence in the problems that may arise.

Their relief to have found someone they believe is as strong and confident as they see themselves lead to mutual respect. They communicate directly and settle disagreements quickly.

Double Eights provide unshakable support building a significant empire. Their confidence in each other allows them to become generous and open-hearted with others.

Potential Trouble

On the flip side, Double Eights are extremely volatile. They put their partner through frequent tests to earn complete control in the relationship. They become competitors and rivals with each other.

The power struggle to be in control will be the center of most conflicts. Unhealthy Eights refuse to back down or be seen as weak.

Eights have short tempers, and at times suspiciousness and paranoia may start setting in. Eights will present tests of loyalty, upping the ante emotionally after each test. They will need to learn to negotiate, or the relationship will eventually wear down.

Eights tend to feel rejected without some kind of power in at least one area. They see this power as an attractant for their partner.

Physical rough-play and verbal assaults can get out of hand because Eights refuse to back down from a conflict and are reluctant to apologize.

Despite their hard exterior, Eights get hurt emotionally very easy and will banish people from their lives over seemingly trivial matters.

Eights need a lot of space and may need to reserve space for themselves that their partner can't cross.

Eights will badger their partner for power until one person finally taps out.

Type Eight with Type Nine

A relationship between Eights and Nines can seem like fire and water. Type Eights have a take-charge attitude other people may look up to and rely on. They are full of vitality and self-confidence.

Nines admire the leadership qualities of Eights. Nines may try to live vicariously through the Nine's positive qualities. Eights enjoy having someone who appreciates their brash leadership. Nines are awed by the Eight's fearlessness and ability to make things happen.

Nines bring a sense of stability and calmness that Eights find comforting and necessary for their wellbeing. Nines encourage Eights to continue in their brashness by showing pride for the Eight bravado.

Despite their persona of having everything under their control, Eights spend a lot of time overcoming hidden demons. They fight to survive and leave their mark on the word. Nines provide a safe harbor for Eights to relax and let their guard down.

Therefore, they tend to teach each other what the other is lacking. Eights teach Nines self-assertion and confidence. Nines attempt to teach Eights when to fight for their values and when to back down and let go.

Both types have strong willpower. They both enjoy simplicity and comfort. Creating a safe retreat from the world is their common goal.

When their goals align, this type of pairing can be powerful, but comfortable at the same time.

Potential Trouble

When Eights and Nines are in unhealthy levels of development, their defenses become opposing factors. Eights push harder, and Nines tend to shut down. Nines will push the Eight away and become unresponsive. Eights become more belligerent and aggressive. Nines respond by going on strike emotionally. Eights will start belittling and threatening the Nine.

Eights will eventually lose interest because they feel Nines are coming between them and their plans. Eights may try to remedy the situation by trying to find something exciting to do, but the Nine will typically respond with a "Why bother?" attitude, causing the Eight to feel rejected and undermined.

Nines perceive unhealthy Eights as too bossy and controlling. Nines think Eights are too selfish and want everything their way.

Nines may think they want someone with a take-charge attitude. But when that attitude is turned against them they rebel and become stubborn.

Eights think the calmness of Nines presents them as a blank slate Eights can mold to their needs. However, Eights are not aware how stubborn Nines can be.

Nines may feel they must protect children or other people they feel would be vulnerable to the Eights violence and hardness.

Rage becomes the cornerstone of the relationship, deteriorating into a battlefield with frequent verbal or physical abuse.

Double Type Nine

As with all double-type relationship, their health level, their wings, and their unique dominant strengths will determine the success or failure of this relationship. A Double Nines relationship is more common to happen naturally than other same-type relationships.

Supportive, gentle, comfortable, hospitable, and quiet are just a few of the qualities that define Nines and their relationship with each other.

Nines typically seem to have unlimited patience and quick to forgive. Nines give each other plenty of affection and undemanding, non-judgmental attention. However, they know when to give each other space when necessary.

Nines perceive each other as kindred spirits who have just the right amount of curiosity and adventure.

Nines do typically prefer routine and familiarity. They will attempt to create a safe haven to protect and prepare their family for life's ups and downs. However, when trouble does come, Nines are steadfast and do not let troubles become a roadblock in their life or in their relationship. Instead, they look for the positive in the circumstance they are facing.

Despite the fact Double Nines are easy-going, they will take whatever means necessary to protect their family. Both partners prefer to take life at their own pace.

Double Nines typically feel comfortable and unpressured within their relationship. This carefree environment is one of the main attractions to this type of relationship.

Mellowness is a tell-tale quality of this type of relationship.

Potential Trouble

The regularity and steadiness Nines prefer can be a double-edged sword for this type of relationship. They fear anything that would intrude or disturb their peace and harmony.

They can seem to be friendly but get stuck in boredom and may gradually drop social connections.

Nines will neglect anyone they feel may be a threat to their relationship.

They may get so caught up in creating harmony in their life and relationship, they be reluctant to bring up important issues. Despite their love for each other, real communication rarely happens. Many times, they keep their frustrations in their head.

Nines in lower levels of development may idealize their partner and relationship. They don't see their partner for who they really are. The majority of their perception of the relationship only happens in their imagination. They may not express their concerns with their partner creating a routine that may eventually threaten the relationship.

Their quietness in their relationship ultimately leads to built-up tension and resentment.

Worry, anxiety, blaming their partner (or other people in their life), and passive-aggressive behavior will undermine their relationship unless they have an outlet to vent.

On the surface, Double Nines may seem to be a perfect match and have an uncanny ability to get along with each other. However, they may actually be suppressive of each other. Their suppressive-ness may kill their vitality and ambition and become characterized by depression with seemingly no cause.

Double Nines may choose to find a way to coexist with little joy or excitement just to keep the relationship alive.

Chapter 12 - What's Your Type?

Some people may read the Enneagram type descriptions and recognize their type right away. Others may have to read on to how their type relates to other personality types before one type resonates with them.

If you have read this far and still have not discovered your type and your wing, the Enneagram Institute provides a full Enneagram profile for only $12. There are other websites which may give an abbreviated reading, but it will not be as detailed. If you have dominant skills from multiple types, it may be best to try the RHETI profile provided by the Enneagram Institute.

Many times, your core personality type will be in your top three test results. Pay attention to the relationship of the types listed. Some of the results may include your stress point and/or your security point. The results may also include your wing type.

Understanding how these types relate to each other can be crucial to determining your true Enneagram type.

Ultimately, you should determine for yourself which Enneagram type you align with the most. Pay attention to the levels of development. Strive for the higher, healthy levels of development.

Conclusion

Thanks for making it through to the end of this book, let's hope it was informative and able to provide you with all the tools you need to achieve your goals of self-discovery.

The next step is to study your types. Study your core type, your wing type, your security point type, and your stress point type. While it is important to avoid labeling those around you, it's also important to study how your type interacts with others. Understanding how each type interacts with others can help you understand other people's behavior. Utilize the information regarding relationships between Enneagram types to develop better ways to approach problems between you and those around you.

There are plenty of books on the Enneagram and personality types on the market, thanks again for choosing this one! Every effort was made to ensure it is full of as much useful information as possible, please enjoy!

Finally, if you found this book useful, please leave a review on Amazon.

www.ingramcontent.com/pod-product-compliance
Lightning Source LLC
Chambersburg PA
CBHW070813280726
48660CB00015B/444